BUSES Magazine
CONTENTS

Editor:
Publisher: Paul Appleton
Design: Matt Chapman, Ian Blaza,
Steve Diggle, Dominique Maynard,
Debbie Walker, Lee Howson
Authors: John Aldridge (JMA),
Michael Baker (MB), Gavin Booth
(GB), Andrew Braddock, Alan Millar
(AM), Peter Rowlands (PR)
Advertising: Sam Clark
Managing Director: Adrian Cox
Commercial Director: Ann Saundry
Marketing: Kirsty Flatt

www.keypublishing.com

Printing: Warners (Midlands) plc,
The Maltings, Bourne, Lincs.
PE10 9PH

ISBN: 978 0 946219 41 4

Registered Office: Key Publishing
Ltd, Units 1-4 Gwash Way Industrial
Estate, Ryhall Road, Stamford,
PE9 1XP.

**Cover: Stagecoach London RM1941
at St Paul's Cathedral, operating
the heritage Routemaster service on
part of route 15.** MARK LYONS

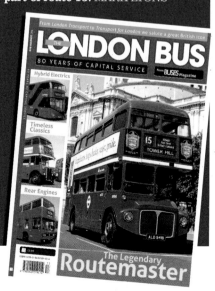

Transport for London began the conversion of its busiest routes to the LT class New Bus for London on 22 June 2013, starting with Metroline-operated 24. This is LT30 at Camden Town on the first day. RUSSELL YOUNG

Part of the city's fabric

Buses change lives. It may sound like a sweeping statement — and you'd be forgiven for thinking I'm biased — but it's true. In London, our buses make a real difference to the way we live, how we get about and the manner in which this remarkable city operates.

From the origins of the London General Omnibus Company to today, this much- loved — sometimes maligned — vehicle has become part of the city's fabric. It is recognised the world over; as iconic as Big Ben, Tower Bridge and our own roundel.

In the 1950s and 1960s the lure of the famous red bus drew thousands of men and women to the capital from the Caribbean and elsewhere, looking forward to futures with London Transport. They helped shape a vibrant city that now speaks more than 300 languages.

Our buses provide a vital service for millions, linking homes to jobs, schools and hospitals in every part of the capital. They form the backbone of our transport network.

London has one of the largest public transport systems in the world, with an 8,500-strong bus fleet, around 700 routes and 19,000 stops. Over the past 80 years, the service, which now accounts for half of all bus journeys in England, has created opportunities for different generations, boosting employment and fuelling the economy.

While most of us sleep, the legions of people who prepare the city for the following day rely on our night buses. Almost half of the passengers who travel on our 24hr routes are going to or from work.

And the network's reach stretches far beyond London. Investment in the capital's transport is safeguarding jobs as, across the UK, people are designing, building and manufacturing on our behalf.

All of this makes me enormously proud. When you consider that more than 90% of the capital's households are just a 5min walk from their local bus stop, it's easy to see how the bus is firmly cemented in London life. And it's open to everyone — our fleet is the world's most accessible.

I've been lucky enough to witness the last part of this story unfold at close quarters. I began my career as a London Transport graduate trainee in 1975 then, via CentreWest and FirstGroup, arrived back at the new Transport for London at the start of 2001, picking up the reins as managing director of Surface Transport. I was honoured to become Commissioner in 2006.

The past decade has been nothing short of a transformation, made possible with the determination of two highly committed Mayors.

Passenger numbers continue to break records and are 60% up on 2000 figures. And when all eyes were on London during the 2012 Olympics and Paralympics, our buses carried a staggering 149million people. The Games were a phenomenal logistical challenge, but we proved the sceptics wrong.

At the same time, customers' satisfaction with buses is increasing and reliability is at its best since records began in 1977.

Given that the city is growing by two bus-loads of people every day, what does the future hold for this iconic vehicle? Further innovation and improvement is the answer, since we simply cannot stand still.

The first New Bus for London arrived in 2012 and is a vehicle of which the capital can be immensely proud. It is modern, efficient and fit for the 21st century. It looks good too. In the words of Frank Pick, the first chief executive of London Transport, 'everyday things

should be not only functional, but pleasing to the eye'.

It's the first bus in more than 50 years to be designed specifically for London's streets and has been created in partnership with Wrightbus and with Heatherwick Studios, the name behind the stunning Olympic cauldron. By 2016, more than 600 will be in service.

The bus makes use of the latest, green diesel-electric hybrid technology. While our fleet is already the cleanest in the UK, we're constantly working to see how new technology can further reduce our impact on the environment.

Bus journeys are becoming easier, more comfortable and more convenient. All vehicles have iBus — audio and visual next-stop information that is particularly valuable to hearing or visually-impaired people.

Accurate, real-time service information is available to customers across a range of platforms. Our travel updates are feeding apps for mobile devices and reaching people in the way that suits

them. Checking when your next bus is due, even before you leave the house, has never been simpler. Live bus information is also being delivered to public locations including hospital waiting rooms, schools and shopping centres.

We're even changing the way people pay for their travel. Four months after the launch of contactless payments on buses, a million journeys had been paid for using a contactless debit, credit or charge card.

From horses to hydrogen, London's bus fleet has been supporting our city for decades. The past 80 years are testament to how fast our industry changes and I believe we have superb foundations on which we can continue to build.

Without the efficient movement of people, our capital could not function properly. Today, the only thing stopping us providing a perfect service is the disruption and congestion on London's road network — and we're working on that too. ∎

Sir Peter Hendy CBE
Commissioner, Transport for London

Ninety years before New Bus for London appeared and the London General Omnibus Company introduced the NS double-decker in 1922. AEC built it 1,804 of them over the next six years and London Transport inherited 1,219 of them in 1933. It set aside one of the last of them, 52-seat NS1995, for preservation after they came out of service in November 1937. It is part of the London Transport Museum collection and took part in the Historic Commercial Vehicle Society's London-Brighton run on 5 May 2013. MARK LYONS

A decade of progress

From its formation in July 1933, London Transport was determined to embrace new ideas and provide a public transport system founded on quality

The London Passenger Transport Board came into being 80 years ago on 1 July 1933, a public board modelled on the few already in existence — the Port of London Authority, Metropolitan Water Board, Central Electricity Board and British Broadcasting Corporation — responsible for all bus, trolleybus, tram and Underground railway services within a 1,550sq mile area and with powers to operate in the immediate area beyond within a wider 1,986sq mile London Passenger Area.

The new board shortened its name to London Transport, which began appearing in bold gold capital letters on the sides of its buses from May 1934.

The London Passenger Transport Act, which received the Royal Assent in April 1933, set out the board's duties to 'secure the provision of an adequate system of passenger transport for the London Passenger Area...while avoiding the provision of unnecessary and wasteful competitive services, to take from time to time such steps as they consider necessary for extending and improving the facilities for passenger transport...in such manner as to provide most efficiently and conveniently for the needs thereof'.

It may have been a public undertaking, but the Act also made clear that it could not be a drain on the public purse. 'It will be the duty of the Board...to fix such fares and charges...to secure that their revenue shall be sufficient to defray all charges which are...required to be defrayed out of the revenues of the Board'. Nor would it be subject to political interference.

One major reason behind its creation was that London's population was growing rapidly and the metropolis was expanding and building huge numbers of new suburban homes to accommodate its new residents. Within a 25mile radius of Charing Cross, the censuses of 1921 and 1931 plotted an increase from 8.3million to 9.2million people, and that would reach 9.9million by the outbreak of World War 2 in September 1939.

There was a good deal of political agreement that something needed to be done, even on what needed to be done. The legislation that led to the 1933 Act had been introduced two years earlier by the then minister of transport, Labour's Herbert Morrison, but was adopted by the coalition that followed the fall of that Labour government and Morrison's temporary move from national to local government.

When his Bill received its second reading, Morrison spelt out why he believed it was vital for London Transport to have a monopoly, telling the House of Commons that if competition between public transport providers involved a needless charge of even a farthing (a 10th of a penny in today's money) per passenger journey, this would still cost £4million a year. That money, he argued, would be better spent on service improvements and reduced fares.

The Underground combine

By far the biggest part of what made up London Transport was the Underground Electric Railways Company of London, a huge combine operating most of the tube and sub-surface Underground railways as well as the London General Omnibus Company, which it had acquired in 1912, and three tram undertakings.

Thanks to resistance to the laying of tram tracks, especially in the West End, buses developed more rapidly and extensively in London than in other large cities in Britain. General had been quick to switch from horse to motor traction and developed and established a subsidiary, the Associated Equipment Company soon better known by its initials AEC, to manufacture its own buses.

The inspirational men in charge of the Underground combine, managing director Lord Ashfield and commercial manager Frank Pick, became chairman and managing director respectively at London Transport.

They made a perfect team, even though they were not temperamentally close. Ashfield was the front man who it is

An LT type AEC Renown six-wheel double-decker and trams at Hammersmith Underground station. LONDON TRANSPORT

said loved nothing better than judging bonny baby contests, conducting the Prince of Wales on a tour of the Underground, shaking hands with all and sundry while Pick, a solicitor by trade, possessed both vision and a meticulous concern for detail.

Pick is credited with London Transport's patronage of art and design — carried forward from the Underground combine — of commissioning material for its publicity from some of the most talented artists of the day, buildings like tube stations, offices, bus garages and stations from eminent architects like Charles Holden, sculpture from Jacob

156 CH. 14. *London Passenger Transport Act, 1933.* 23 GEO. 5.

CHAPTER 14.

An Act to provide for the establishment of a Passenger Transport Board for an area to be known as the London Passenger Transport Area, which shall comprise certain portions of the London Traffic Area and of the districts adjacent thereto, and for the transfer to that Board of various transport undertakings and interests; to make other provisions with respect to traffic in the said area; and for purposes connected with the matters aforesaid. [13th April 1933.]

BE it enacted by the King's most Excellent Majesty, by and with the advice and consent of the Lords Spiritual and Temporal, and Commons, in this present Parliament assembled, and by the authority of the same, as follows:—

PART I.

CONSTITUTION AND GENERAL POWERS OF LONDON PASSENGER TRANSPORT BOARD.

1.—(1) For the purposes of this Act there shall, as soon as may be after the passing of this Act, be established a public authority to be called the London Passenger Transport Board (in this Act referred to as "the Board"), consisting of a chairman and six other members from time to time appointed by a body (in

The Act of Parliament that created London Transport. JMA COLLECTION

PART I. —*cont.* this Act referred to as "the Appointing Trustees") consisting of the following persons:—

the chairman of the London County Council;

a representative of the Advisory Committee (as hereinafter in this Act defined);

the chairman of the Committee of London Clearing Bankers;

the president of the Law Society;

the president of the Institute of Chartered Accountants in England and Wales; and

in the case of appointments to fill vacancies in the Board at any time after the first constitution of the Board, the chairman of the Board or some other member of the Board nominated by the Board for the purpose.

The appointments to be made by the Appointing Trustees shall be made after consultation with such persons as they may think fit.

(2) The chairman and other members of the Board shall be persons who have had wide experience, and have shown capacity, in transport, industrial, commercial or financial matters or in the conduct of public affairs and, in the case of two members, shall be persons who have had not less than six years experience in local government within the London Passenger Transport Area.

(3) A Member of the Commons House of Parliament shall be disqualified for being appointed or being a member of the Board.

(4) A member of the Board shall hold office for such term, not less than three years nor longer than seven years, as the Appointing Trustees may determine at the time of his appointment:

Provided that a member may resign his office by notice in writing under his hand given to the Minister of Transport (in this Act referred to as "the Minister").

(5) Where any member of the Board is absent from the meetings of the Board for more than six months consecutively, except for some reason approved by the Minister, or becomes bankrupt or makes a composition or arrangement with his creditors, the Minister shall forthwith declare the office to be vacant, and shall notify

Epstein and a rigorous approach to a corporate style based on elegant and clear typography.

The new organisation adopted the Underground's bulls eye roundel as its highly recognisable logo.

Ashfield and Pick believed that it was not enough for a public transport service simply to be efficient, but for it to appear to be of the highest quality, for its users to feel that they are travelling in vehicles and on a system that is at least on a par with the comfort and good taste that

they would bestow on their own private property if they could afford it, and that it should appear to be at the cutting edge of modernity.

The Underground brought around 4,300 buses to London Transport from General and its subsidiaries, together with the tram undertakings of London United, Metropolitan Electric and South Metropolitan. London United also had the beginnings of what would grow quickly into the United Kingdom's biggest trolleybus undertaking, 61 double-

deckers that had replaced trams in May 1931.

In all, London Transport acquired 2,630 electric trams in 1933, making it by some margin the biggest operator of them in the British Isles. Most came from local authorities, especially London County Council. The others were from boroughs and urban district councils in Croydon, East Ham, West Ham, Barking, Bexley, Erith, Ilford and Walthamstow. They were concentrated in north, east and south-east London.

Within the Metropolitan Police area — the Met held huge sway over the regulation of London's buses then, having allocated the route numbers and specifying what could or could not be fitted to a London bus — a further 57 bus operators provided services.

Only Thomas Tilling — 369 buses and three garages in south-east and south London at Bromley, Catford and Croydon — came anywhere near approaching the size of General. It owed the size of its bus operation to a pre-World War 1 agreement with General to guarantee it a limited share of the London bus market. The Tilling connection survives to the present day with the two-letter abbreviation on the sides of buses at these three garages starting with a T for Tilling (TB for Bromley, TC for Croydon and TL for Catford, the L being for Lewisham where Tilling based its buses before 1920).

The other independent operators collectively had 277 buses of assorted makes and models — mainly Leyland and Dennis double-deckers — and accounted for just 6% of passengers carried within the Met area.

London Transport took over Tilling's buses in October 1933 and the independents within what became its Central Area had followed by early December 1934. The 1933 Act gave London Transport compulsory purchase powers over these businesses, but the owners could either accept the terms on offer from the new board or appeal to an arbitration tribunal if they felt that their enterprises were being undervalued. Payment was a combination of cash and stock in London Transport, so although the new board was a public body it also had private shareholders.

After General, the largest operator taken over was Tilling, whose ST class AEC Regents had open stairs and older-style bodies that proved to be structurally poor. JMA COLLECTION

Always on the quest for improvements, London Transport built this streamlined STL type AEC Regent in 1935 with an enclosed radiator and full-width glazed front. The raked front anticipated the appearance of the RT four years later and the enclosed radiator the Routemaster of 19 years later. Originally STL857, it was renumbered STF1 and ran like this only until 1938 when it was rebuilt with the normal half cab and exposed radiator, after which it became STL857 again. J. F. HIGHAM

In the General's footsteps

Within the Central Area — the biggest part of its domain — London Transport continued to use the red livery that General had applied to its motorbuses since 1907. In the Country Area beyond (see p12), they would be green.

Indeed, hardly surprisingly given the proportion of services it already operated, there was a huge level of continuity from General to London Transport, not least that Chiswick Works would go on building most of the bodywork for its new buses and the close association over chassis development and production would continue with AEC, which General had formed in the early days of motorbus development when it was the largest bus operator in Britain and it had decided that no commercially available chassis was what it required.

While few if any Chiswick bodies were built for outsiders, AEC freely engaged in also building for the open market and had for a time been in a joint venture, Associated Daimler, with the Daimler company in Coventry. Thus when London Transport was set up, almost all its fleet was AEC, plus some Associated Daimlers.

There had been numerous high-level discussions, investigations and meetings with Leyland from 1926 onwards for a merger but no firm proposal ever emerged. Later, the Underground combine had also discussed a sale to Ford Motor Company.

London Transport's monopoly position meant that AEC had to be separated from it, and it was given an independent life from 1 November 1933. London Transport then gave it a 10-year contract for the supply of 90% of its motorbus chassis and spares.

By July 1933, the latest London version of the AEC Regent — classed STL by General — was already entering the fleet and is described on p16. The new organisation inherited 1,226 three-axle LT-class AEC Renowns (including 200 single-deckers) from General, substantial numbers of the shorter ST type Regent and around 400 T type AEC Regal single-deckers, as well as smaller numbers of other types.

A less welcome statistic was to be that it still had 1,219 of the dated 1,804 NS double-deckers built between 1922 and 1928. Remarkably it managed to see off the last of them on 30 November 1937.

Not only were buses being replaced, but engineering advances were incorporated into the new buses. Petrol engines gave way to more economical and durable diesel, transmission changed from heavy manual gearboxes and bodywork was made stronger and lighter.

London Transport's impressive headquarters at 55 Broadway, built above St James's Park Underground station. Latterly headquarters of London Underground, this listed building is to be sold for conversion to flats. LONDON TRANSPORT

Lord Ashfield

Frank Pick

Eight Park Royal-bodied Leyland Cub coaches with large luggage compartments and a raised seating area over the back operated the Inter Station connection between mail-line railway terminals from 1936. They were painted blue and primrose. LONDON TRANSPORT

TF1, the prototype Leyland Tiger FEC coach with underfloor engine. The others of this type had a less elaborate driver's cab structure that blended into the rest of the bodywork. D. W. K. JONES

Innovation from Leyland

The remaining 10% of the new chassis business went to Leyland, a significant proportion of which involved some highly innovative designs developed by operator and manufacturer. Together with the RT double-decker (see p34), they show how determined London Transport was to push the boundaries of bus design and lead the way for others to follow.

The first of these was the TF class, an underfloor-engined version of Leyland's Tiger coach or single-deck bus that appeared in October 1937. Until then, all British buses had an engine at the front, with the driver sitting either in a separate cab alongside or in the passenger saloon behind the engine.

Things were done differently in some other countries, notably the United States, where there were 'pusher' buses with the engine at the back and 'pancake' designs with a horizontal engine under

the floor. With both these approaches, it was possible to have more seats, and Leyland was keen to import these ideas to the UK.

The TF was the first British attempt at a 'pancake' bus. Termed the Tiger FEC (for Flat Engine Coach), it still sat the driver in a separate cab over the front wheels but by not having an engine alongside it made his working environment quieter and afforded superior visibility to the pavement side of the road.

These coaches were developed primarily for the Country Area's Green Line coach services, the prototype with 34-seat Leyland-built body being followed in 1939 by another 75, all with bodywork built at Chiswick and a further dozen private hire coaches with Park Royal bodywork. Eleven of the coaches were destroyed in a bombing raid in 1940.

The other innovative Leyland was a 'pusher', a rear-engined version of the small Cub chassis of which London Transport had bought 112 new between 1934 and 1936, six of them with raised rear roof and luggage compartment for an Inter Station service for railway passengers crossing London. The REC (Rear Engine Cub) looked like a scaled-down version of the TF, but was lower and had its 4.4litre diesel engine in a compartment at the back. While the TF had an AEC preselector gearbox, this had a manual 'crash' 'box.

This was classed CR by London Transport and the prototype arrived at the end of 1937. Forty-eight more followed in 1939/40, all arriving after the outbreak of war, for Central Area and Country Area routes. All had 20-seat bodies built at Chiswick. Leyland built no more rear-engined buses until 1953 and it would be 1965 before London Transport bought any.

Trams to trolleybuses

One of London Transport's biggest prewar bus achievements was its replacement of large parts of the tram networks with electric trolleybuses. It undertook this as part of the first of a projected series of five-year plans, the 1935-40 New Works Programme, which also embraced some ambitious extensions of the Underground.

London United's conversion of Kingston routes to trolleybuses had delivered a 15% reduction in operating costs. Obsolete trams could be scrapped and worn-out track lifted without the need for its replacement or continuing maintenance. On the other hand, the power generation and distribution network for the electricity needed to power the trams still had a lot of viable life left in it and could be used for trolleybuses. Further, as the 1930s edged closer to war, having a power system that relied on home-produced coal rather than imported oil was a further factor in favour of electric traction.

Unlike trams, trolleybuses could steer around obstacles in the immediate vicinity of the overhead wiring and pull into the kerbside, which made life safer for their passengers as other road traffic grew in volume.

Having gained powers to operate them, starting in October 1935 and ending in June 1940, the trolleybus network grew to 68 routes over 255miles, mainly north of the Thames and especially in an arc stretching from Hounslow, Uxbridge and Edgware to Ilford and Barking, but with pockets of operation in place of trams dotted between south-west and south-east London. This made use of £13million of power supply infrastructure that might otherwise have been lost.

By 1939, 1,411 trolleybuses were covering 236 route miles and carrying 571million passengers. The tram system was down to 1,316 cars carrying 516million passengers over 135 route miles. London Transport's had already become the world's largest trolleybus system of its age, and later reached a peak of 1,811 vehicles.

There were plans to purchase over 1,000 more trolleybuses to replace the trams south of the Thames. The outbreak of war certainly halted that possibility, but resistance to trolleybuses was growing even before that, especially from those who believed that their overhead wires disfigured the streetscapes. Indeed, Westminster City Council and some other local authorities had prevented their operation in much of the heart of London.

A separate Tram & Trolleybus Department looked after electric street transport and while the trolleybuses — all double-deckers, all but one of them with six wheels — also were red and cream, the application of the colours differed from motorbuses, the bodywork bore no resemblance to that of their petrol and diesel counterparts and other features like destination and route

number displays were quite different. There was no obligation to buy 90% of these vehicles from AEC, orders being divided more evenly between Leyland and AEC.

The 1937 bus strike

The first years of London Transport saw its motorbuses grow in number and carry significantly more passengers as the population of London grew. In 1933/34, the board's first year, 5,976 buses and coaches carried 1.9billion passengers. By 1938/39, 6,389 buses carried 2.2billion.

The number of passengers dipped from 2.1billion in 1936/37 to 2billion in 1937/38, thanks to a strike by the 27,000

Central Area bus crews for most of May 1937, taking services off for the duration of the major public event of the year, the coronation of King George VI and Queen Elizabeth. The strike was in pursuit of a reduction in the working day, which London Transport said it could not afford but later partly conceded.

It cost the board £700,000 in lost revenue, even though trams and trolleybuses — where they operated — carried 60% more passengers than usual and the number of Underground passengers doubled.

Testing as this experience had been, far tougher times lay ahead as London Transport prepared for the onset of war. ■ **AM**

The business end of CR16, a preserved example of one of the rear-engined Leyland Cubs, now on extended loan to the London Bus Museum. AM

Two 1935-built trolleybuses on the isolated south-east London part of the network. On the left is a B2 class Leyland with Brush bodywork. On the right is a C1 class AEC with Metro-Cammell body. LONDON TRANSPORT

Country buses & Green Line coaches

With London expected to keep growing outwards as its population increased, London Transport enjoyed rights to operate buses and coaches over large parts of south-east England

For 37 years, besides the world famous red buses London Transport's Country Bus & Coach department served the surrounding towns and villages of the rapidly growing capital city.

Its green buses covered an area measured as a 25 or 30mile radius of Charing Cross. Boundaries ran 60miles from Hitchin in the north to Crawley in the south, 40miles from Slough in the west to Grays and Gravesend in the east.

Boundary towns included Harlow, Tonbridge, Guildford and High Wycombe. London Transport could go a half mile outside most boundary towns, but had unrestricted rights to run farther to a few places including Aylesbury, Maidenhead, Windsor and Forest Row, and had restricted rights to run out to Tilbury and Tunbridge Wells.

The total area covered by the London Passenger Area was 1,986sq miles and within that 1,550sq miles was the Special Area for which it had monopoly powers.

Preserved Green Line AEC Regal T504, one of 266 class 10T10 coaches built at Chiswick in 1938/39

Much of that 'outer ring of countryside' was already generally served by London General Country Services plus what it described as 'no man's lands' needed traffic commissioners' approval for its routes.

London General Country Services was a then recent name for what had been the East Surrey Traction Company. That company was based at Reigate and run by Arthur H. Hawkins. It had signed a kind of area agreement over territory with the London General Omnibus Company back in 1914 that defined the A25 road between Guildford and Sevenoaks as the boundary, with East Surrey running to the south of it.

A bigger agreement in 1921 was for it to develop services outside the Metropolitan Police Area for which London General would provide buses, equipment and garages. In 1928, the four main line railway companies had received powers to invest in bus companies, a move that worried General, probably because there had already been skirmishes between the two over rail or tube expansion plans in south-west London.

So it bought East Surrey outright in June 1928. The name changed to London General Country Services in 1932, just before General transferred services to it to the north and east of London previously run on its behalf by the National Omnibus & Transport. This comprised buses and garages at Watford, Ware, Hatfield, Luton, Bishops Stortford and Romford.

Takeovers begin

From 1 July 1933, London Transport began taking over operators or parts of their operations within its area. Its Country Area was based at Reigate and continued to be run by Arthur Hawkins for many years. Livery changed from the red of London General Country Services to green, with a black stripe below the windows: staff uniforms were green too.

Traffic and engineering operations were put into five districts: South-east, South-west, Western, North-west and North-east, each with its own local management.

Some of the well-known bigger bus companies lost territory, such as Aldershot & District and Thames Valley Traction.

A particular loser was Maidstone & District, which had to hand-over its Dartford and Gravesend garages along with 43 buses and 12 coaches on 18 routes. Here and also at Grays passengers lost out, with useful through routes being split. For example, a Maidstone & District service between Dartford, Gravesend and the Medway Towns was severed.

Another side-effect was felt south-west of London where an independent operator ran two routes between Staines Bridge and Virginia Water. Buses had worked out on one route and looped in

With help from the General, East Surrey Traction became the dominant operator in country south of London, but changed its name to London General Country Services the year before London Transport was formed. This ST type AEC Regent was one of 60 bodied by Ransomes, Sims & Jefferies of Ipswich for country work. Unfortunately the blueprints supplied to the bodybuilder were of the original Chiswick-built single square-cabbed ST instead of the curved-cab production batch that had followed. JMA COLLECTION

service round Knowle Hill to return on the other. Both routes started from the south side of Staines Bridge, because being outside the Metropolitan Police area the buses avoided the onerous conditions on vehicle specification that London's red buses had to endure.

That loop had to be lost, as Knowle Hill was outside the London Transport area. It remained unserved until after World War 2.

London Transport's compulsory acquisition of independents went ahead: these businesses could either settle on

Forward-entrance STLs were the favoured double-decker for the Country Area prewar. JMA COLLECTION

agreed terms laid down by the legislation or appeal over valuations placed on them and go to arbitration, which delayed their takeover. Many were very small operators running 14- or 20-seat buses — the latter was the maximum allowed for operation without a conductor.

For example, 10 operators taken over in Slough in 1933 and 1934 had 28 buses between them, and three of them each had just one bus. In total, the Country Area took vehicles of 31 different makes, including rarities such as Brockway, Manchester and Overland. Many of the acquired buses were too small or too decrepit and were never used.

As far as possible, usable buses were grouped together in particular garages to ease the spares and maintenance nightmare. Some 'unwanteds' from the Central Area were also transferred to the country, such as the only Maudslay double-decker from the Gordon Omnibus Company of Leyton, which ended up at Windsor.

Overhauling the fleet

Overhauling this much-enlarged fleet of buses and coaches continued at Reigate until 1935, then moved to the Chiswick Works (see p52). Chiswick added fleetnumbers for the first time in a somewhat arbitrary fashion based on the first letter of the registration plate. Thus the very first AEC Regent, registration UU 6610, gained the highest fleet

number in its class as ST1139.

Apart from a small batch of lowheight double-deckers, AEC Regents with Weymann bodies later numbered STL1044-1055, there were no deliveries of new country buses until 1935. The country bus fleet, like that of central buses, included some open-top double-deckers, but the double-deck mix was simpler and easier to handle.

A particular need was for covered accommodation and London Transport was quick off the mark, building the first new one, at Epping, by September 1934. Others followed in the same basic attractive architectural style, the prototype being Dorking, actually completed in 1932. One of the best and best known, complete with bus station in front, was St Albans, only recently demolished and replaced by housing.

World War 2 brought an enormous increase in vehicle requirements as people moved out of London and numerous factories were established for aircraft production and other war work. The number of passengers carried between September 1939 and the end of the war almost doubled.

Later in the war, to save fuel no buses ran on Sunday mornings except for factory workers. For example, on route 353 (Berkhamsted-Amersham-Slough-Windsor) there was an 06.32 departure from Amersham to Slough, which returned to Amersham at 07.46. The next bus from Amersham was not until 12.17, and the next from Slough was at 13.49.

The number of standing passengers allowed was increased and if double-

deckers could be substituted for single-deckers this too was done. Also numerous routes worked by Leyland Cub C-class single-deckers were upped to full-sized single-deckers with a conductor.

One unusual feature was that newer STL double-deckers were taken off some trunk routes of an interurban nature and replaced by older and smaller STs because the STLs when heavily laden could not keep to time, whereas thirsty petrol-engined STs could. Some of these routes were later the first to gain new RT double-deckers.

Green Line coaches

The coach part of the department operated the Green Line limited stop services connecting the surrounding towns with central London, worked by what were described as coaches but were really rather superior single-deck buses. General had begun them in 1929 and they developed very rapidly. Officialdom took a very dim view of them and imposed a deadline of 9 February 1931 after which it became extremely difficult to start any new ones in London.

Both Green Line and several independents were successful before then, and General bought out many of the independents before London Transport was formed. Most were or became cross-London routes, but picking up passengers inside the Metropolitan Police Area was strictly controlled and limited.

A central London coach station, off Poland Street in Soho, south of Oxford Street, had opened at Christmas 1930 but at the request of the Metropolitan Police and Westminster City Council it was closed in October 1933. Running 27 or more coaches an hour through the narrow Soho streets had caused problems.

Nevertheless by the late 1930s around 35 routes were operating to such places as Tunbridge Wells, Dorking, Windsor, High Wycombe, Luton, Brentwood and Tilbury. They needed 350 coaches on most days, but Sunday duplication added another 150 to the requirements.

Besides the TF class Leylands described in the previous chapter, two sets of prewar Green Line coaches worthy of mention are AEC Regals known to London Transport as the 9T9 and 10T10. The 50 type 9T9 were ordered in 1936 with 30-seat Weymann bodies. The chassis was to virtually the same specification as the STL double-decker with 7.7litre engine but the body had a restyled front with integral wing assembly and bonnet and front bumper.

Weymann also built the bodies for 24 high-specification private hire coaches for the Central and Country Areas, for which the six-wheel AEC Renown chassis was chosen to reduce wheelarch intrusion. Coded LTC, they had petrol engines, fluid flywheels and preselector gearboxes, the engines being overhauled units from Chiswick while AEC supplied new 8.8diesels for six-wheel LT-class double-deckers. The LTCs had individual luxury seats, opening roof and a radio, the latter quite an innovation.

The 9T9 lacked the power needed for Green Line work, and the 10T10 new build in 1938-39 of 266 coaches set high standards. These had a new pot cavity direct injection version of AEC's 8.8litre engine, built under licence from Leyland. It was powerful yet quiet running. They had Chiswick-built bodies with more metal in their structure though still composite, and a simpler front-end layout. They were highly regarded by both staff and passengers. ■ **JMA**

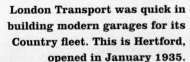

London Transport was quick in building modern garages for its Country fleet. This is Hertford, opened in January 1935. LONDON TRANSPORT

The short-lived Poland Street coach station in Soho, with art deco frontage and rather more garage-like facilities inside. JMA COLLECTION

The STL

Above: Inside the restored top deck of STL2377. GAVIN BOOTH

Right: STL2377, new in November 1937, has been fully restored as part of the London Bus Museum collection. MARK LYONS

London Transport's standard prewar double-decker was the STL, like the ST before it and the RT that followed a vehicle based on the AEC Regent. Most had bodies built at Chiswick Works in west London.

If ST stood for 'Short Type' then this was 'ST Lengthened', as a change in regulations permitted it to be 1ft longer at 26ft. The three-axle AEC Renown, which had been favoured for a while for higher-capacity buses, was the LT, whether single-deck or double-deck. The Regent's single-deck equivalent, the AEC Regal, was class T.

General had introduced the first STLs in January 1933, six months before London Transport was formed and the last of an initial 100 60-seaters were delivered to the new board, followed by 400 56-seaters of much changed appearance with a sloping but rather flat front.

These had an AEC petrol engine of 6.1litres that was virtually unchanged from that used in the ST. There were numerous experiments: among them some with 'crash' gearboxes, others with preselector gearboxes (the driver selected the gear than used a 'clutch' pedal to engage that gear) with or without fluid flywheels.

Just 11 chassis had the new AEC diesel engine that was desperately wanted. The problem was that AEC's 8.8litre diesel (they called them oil engines then) was too long to fit an STL, and AEC was only developing a shorter length engine of 7.7litre capacity. All those petrol engines on these new STLs were not new but a swap. They were overhauled units taken from older six-wheel LTs. In turn AEC provided, loose, 8.8diesels, which Chiswick Works then fitted to existing LTs.

There also were STL types acquired

from Thomas Tilling's London business. These had interiors far superior to Chiswick's products, with mahogany window surrounds, deeper seat cushions and lightweight tubular seat frames. Tilling's engineering meanness showed through even then: they had a downrated AEC engine with sleeved pistons to give a volume of only 5.1litres but lacked starter motors — drivers had to swing the handle each time. An early move by London Transport was to fit starter motors and later it changed the engines.

Also taken over — in November 1933 — were five Regents from Charles Pickup, which attracted considerable attention as they were open-toppers although the chassis dated from 1932. They had crash gearboxes and a larger AEC engine which with their light weight gave them quite a turn of speed. Pickup had used them on summer Sundays and bank holidays on route 37 to Richmond, where they

could attract high passenger loads. But Chiswick replaced their upper decks with new ones of almost standard STL design.

Big step forward

November 1934 saw a big step forward in London bus design with the unveiling of STL609, the first standard STL. The first 150 were followed by over 2,000 of generally similar — but slightly improving — body design and its general outline was copied by most other bodybuilders.

There was a gentle curve across the width of the front and a neat curve in the other plane ran from the bottom of the cab front to the roof. There was a sharper, but arguably neater curve to the rear of the body but that feature was not repeated on either the RT or the Routemaster.

Putting the Autovac fuel pump under the bonnet also improved the frontal appearance. The interior was a particular

improvement on the grey drabness of previous buses. A change to a lighter colour halfway up the window pillars made a big difference, with the curved profile of the lower deck ceiling another feature.

London Transport's Country Area had a fairly separate existence until 1935 but its one early order — in 1933 — was for 12 lowheight forward-entrance Regents with 8.8litre diesel engines and Weymann metal-framed bodies. Popular with passengers, they had a long life, four being relicensed for use as extras during the 1953 Coronation.

Eighty-five Chiswick-built STLs for the Country Area also had forward entrances; they had parcel shelves over the rear wheelarches and only 48 seats. Wartime vast increases in numbers travelling in the Country Area saw the shelves replaced by inward-facing seats for two on each side. Such an increase was not possible

on the later batch of 89, which had almost identical but metal-framed Weymann bodies. They were heavier, but the bodies proved sturdier and trouble-free.

Something different again, this time from Chiswick, was a batch of 40 to replace the special covered-top NSs used for routes through the two Thames tunnels. They had been General's first buses with enclosed staircases.

The Rotherhithe and Blackwall Tunnel roadways were only 15ft 9in wide, the STLs each 7ft 6in. They had heavily domed roofs to clear the tunnel lighting and this necessitated a change to the top of the staircase, which reduced the length of the offside lower deck-inward facing seat and cut capacity to 55. The rear of the body was tapered and tyres had reinforced sidewalls to withstand constant rubbing against the tunnel kerbs.

A ride through the tunnels was a very different experience. It usually began with the driver standing up in his seat and reaching out to fold inwards the offside rear-view mirror. There was a continuous high-pitched and loud noise from the tunnel ventilation equipment and very tight corners could only be negotiated by one large vehicle in one direction at a time.

Late in 1936 came the first STLs with the front roof route number box, a feature that many thought made them the most attractive of the class. There were 360 of these, plus the 40 tunnel STLs, taking the class up to 2,013, to be followed by 175 STL bodies from Park Royal. These were virtually identical to standard ones, but under the skin had metal-frame construction, which sadly did not stand the test of time.

Part of the post-war SRT programme – described in the RT profile starting on p34 — was to see bodies from many STL chassis used to replace rotten Park Royal ones. They were followed by another 300 plus Chiswick-bodied STLs.

Petrol to diesel

The final prewar batch of 130 STLs had a new AEC A173 direct injection engine that ran at lower revs, with flexible engine mounts and also automatic brake adjustors. This engine was also used in a programme to convert 286 'leaning back' petrol STLs to diesel along with another 400 six-wheel LT double-deckers.

Total cost of this work worked out at £425 per bus, but the annual fuel saving was computed at over £260 a year. Perhaps because of all this expense, although fitting the new engine necessitated raising the front of the body

Standard STL2509 traversing flood water at Westminster in November 1938. Note the experimental twin windscreen wipers. JMA COLLECTION

The general outline of a standard STL was used for illustrations on the back of a form for drivers to fill in when reporting a collision. They had to mark affected areas on the drawing in red ink. JMA COLLECTION

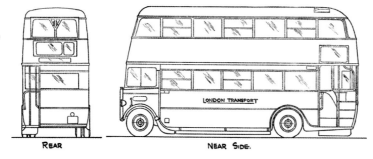

REAR   NEAR SIDE.

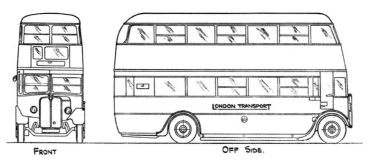

FRONT   OFF SIDE.

slightly, no attempt was made to balance their appearance, which accentuated their 'leaning back' look. There was a later plan to convert existing STL, Q and the 50 recent Weymann Green Line Regals to direct injection for under £50 each, but the war slowed the programme and some were never done.

Next double-deck orders were for the new RT, but wartime need for more buses was partly met by London receiving 34 'unfrozen' AEC Regents with crash gearboxes. 'Unfrozen' buses were ones on which construction had started but then stopped because of other war needs: their completion was now authorised.

Chiswick built the bodies to an austere specification, with a lack of internal trim and other savings. Fourteen were built to full height and the remaining 20 of lowbridge layout around 1ft lower than

The first order placed by the new Country Bus department was for 12 low-height AEC Regents with Weymann bodies for Godstone garage. They were the first diesels in the Country fleet and became STL1044 to 1055. JMA COLLECTION

STL963, one of the forward-entrance Country Area buses with Weymann bodywork. The open platform was designed to be relatively draught-free. LONDON TRANSPORT

Specially designed STL1866 emerging from the Blackwall Tunnel when new in April 1937. LONDON TRANSPORT

'Leaning back' STL441 of June 1934, also part of the London Bus Museum collection.

The distinctive rear of an STL with Y-shaped mouldings in the top deck emergency door. This is STL441.

the standard height, wartime needs overcoming the police previous reluctance of the Metropolitan Police to allow this.

To explain, the vast majority of London double-deckers were 'highbridge' vehicles, with around 15 pairs of forward facing seats upstairs either side of a central gangway.

The layout of lowbridge buses was pretty unsatisfactory until new designs appeared in the 1950s, as the top-deck gangway — the only part upstairs where adults could stand at anything like their full height — was on the driver's side. Its floor was lower than most of the bottom deck ceiling, so passengers on that side downstairs risked bumping their heads when they stood up to get off.

Upstairs, the seats were in rows of four (just three in the back row) close to the roof, so people sitting nearest the windows on the pavement side might have to squeeze past those next to the gangway while adopting the pose of Quasimodo, Victor Hugo's *Hunchback of Notre Dame*. Conductors shuffled along the gangway, with passengers stretching across to pay their fares.

Last burst of life

When the 'unfrozen' STLs arrived, Chiswick was already building 17 highbridge bodies to replace war losses but material and staff shortages made production slow. So, many of the new chassis gained spare bodies of various types from the STL float, the most notable being two that received original 60-seater bodies. In the 1950s one was the subject of an unsuccessful private preservation appeal.

All the lowbridge bodies went on to existing chassis emerging from overhaul: they retained the STL family appearance. The bodies were mounted on whatever newly overhauled chassis were available at the time.

The STL had one final burst of life when the last 20, STL2682 to STL2701, were received in 1946. These were allocated to the Country Area and their AEC Regent II chassis (the prewar Regent with minor modifications) had Weymann's new postwar-style provincial bodies, complete with polished wood finishers to windows and other touches soon eliminated by brown paint on first overhaul.

They were kept only until 1955, then sold to three municipal bus operators — 10 to Dundee, six to Grimsby and four to Widnes — as London Transport could by then afford to sell all of its non-standard buses. ■ **JMA**

THE Q TYPE

George John Rackham had not long settled down to his job as chief engineer of AEC and designing the Regal, Regent and Renown chassis, before producing a revolutionary new design — the Q Type.

It was as innovative in its day as was Leyland's first rear-engined double-deck Atlantean in the 1950s. Instead of the driver being beside the engine, as in all other large bus designs, the Q had the engine behind the driver on the offside

and mounted as low as practical to allow a long inward-facing seat above it.

General was suitably impressed and for a short time placed the prototype single-decker on prestigious route 11, among all the double-deckers.

While the Q was innovative as a single-decker, some of its double-deckers, built in penny numbers, were even more advanced, with the driver ahead of the front axle and an entrance doorway opposite him. London bought two, and two more with central entrances (a layout

that was a bit of an obsession with the country bus people).

The Q's mechanical specification was unique in employing a reverse-rotation AEC engine, with a different firing sequence. Radiator and engine were immediately behind the offside front wheel. The rear axle was positioned farther to the rear than normal and there were single rear wheels — which made them much more skittish buses on snowy or icy roads.

The double-deckers saw limited service

Left: Double-deck Q2 with Metro-Cammell body when new in 1934. Although this official photograph shows it operating route 77 from Chalk Farm garage, Q2 and Q3 operated on other routes from other garages, transferring to the Country Area in 1937.
LONDON TRANSPORT

Right: Q1 in its original form on route 11E in its earliest days in central London.
JMA COLLECTION

Left: Q83, new in 1935 and restored to Central Area red but showing a Country Area destination, is in the London Bus Museum collection.

Right: A driver in his summer uniform shows the engine location of Q1.
JMA COLLECTION

in central London, and then all four double-deckers, plus a later six-wheel double-decker intended for Green Line use but never so used, ended up as country buses at Hertford. All were taken out of service soon after the outbreak of war, and sold off after the war, most then working for small independent operators.

The big breakthrough for the Q was the country bus order for 100 — plus two more slightly later — with distinctive 37-seat central-entrance bodywork by the Birmingham Railway Carriage & Wagon Company. Delivered in 1935, they had an inward–facing seat for two opposite the driver, but complaints by them about nearside visibility (probably) or structural problems (possibly but unlikely) led to all being rebuilt with a conventional bulkhead behind the driver and seating only 35, a figure that could have been achieved with a conventional single-decker with a front engine.

There was a door into the cab in the centre of the bulkhead, and in later years a loop of string was often hung inside the doorway. Attached to the door catch to hold the door open, it made conductor-

driver conversation easier. Several of this batch of Qs were fitted with heaters and a front grille for Green Line use for a year or two.

The next batch, of 80 buses with 37-seat Park Royal bodies, were the most innovative, with the driver ahead of the front axle, and an open doorway opposite him. Apparently intended for Central Area use, several moved to the Country Area in return for country ones.

Apparently the chairman of the traffic commissioners, a very powerful man in those days, took exception to the Qs, permitting use on only some routes for the central-entrance ones, whereas he only sanctioned front-entrance ones for other routes. Perhaps that was why London Transport's enthusiasm for the Q faded. The last production batch was for 50 for full-time Green Line use. They seated only 32. They had the usual inward facing seat over the engine, but with armrests for each passenger.

All three types of Q remained in use until replaced by new RFs in the 1950s, but a bizarre twist to the story was the use of some Green Line ones already out of service for disposal. At union instigation, they were relicensed and transferred to Muswell Hill for central bus use.

They replaced six-wheeled single-deck LT Renowns with disintegrating bodies: passengers also had complained about having to keep up their umbrellas inside those buses in wet weather.

Some Qs were sold off for further use, mainly with building contractors, while a few went overseas. ■ **JMA**

Green Line Q195 with Park Royal body.
LONDON TRANSPORT

Route 1

London's bus route number 1 is a bit of a puzzle. Given its supremacy in the route-numbering hierarchy, you might imagine that it would go somewhere pretty important. Well, to some extent it does; but it does so almost surreptitiously; it keeps its head down.

Its southern destination, Canada Water, is also teasing. It sounds (and indeed proves to be) trendy: south-east London's answer to Docklands proper, on the other side of the Thames. But the rest of the route is quite another matter, following a meandering trail through a mixed landscape of Victorian and 20th century developments: mostly residential, with terraced houses from many periods sitting cheek by jowl with high-rise flats and sometimes shops.

The 1 is operated by Go-Ahead London General, thanks to a complex history of

route swapping between bus companies, and the buses themselves are mostly Volvo B7TL double-deckers with Wright Eclipse Gemini bodies, still in full company livery of red with a grey skirt surmounted by yellow lining. However, Alexander Dennis Enviro400s also pop up on the route from time to time, in this case in Transport for London's allover red.

Most Volvos have London's latest single-line destination screen, which is certainly easy to read, but denies travellers the

detail offered by the few that still have multi-destination screens.

At its northern extremity, the route starts just beyond the eastern end of Oxford Street — actually in a nondescript side street called Earnshaw Street. Officially the terminus is called Tottenham Court Road, though the buses don't actually set foot there; they loiter under the shadow of Centre Point, the 1960s office tower, then head off eastwards along New Oxford Street towards Holborn.

A northbound 1 in Kingsway, where the Strand Underpass emerges from part of the old Kingsway Subway for trams.

Left: A southbound number 1 on Waterloo Bridge, passing the South Bank complex. This Wright-bodied Volvo was new to East Thames Buses, which Go-Ahead acquired in 2009.

Classic downstream view from the top of a number 1 of the Thames towards St Paul's, Blackfriars Bridge and an ever-changing City skyline.

But the 1 is really a north-south route. It once ran from Willesden in north-west London to Lewisham and Bromley in the south-east. So it turns south at the first opportunity, about half a mile on.

Then it heads down Kingsway: wide but forbidding, flanked by early 20th century office blocks and not really a place for pedestrians (except round Holborn Underground at the north end). Along the centre are the remnants of the tunnel that used to take trams under the Aldwych, and part of which is now a one-way road underpass.

After mingling with a kerfuffle of east-west bus routes in the Aldwych, a semi-circular one-way system characterised by embassies, theatres and two churches (one by Wren), the 1 breaks free with a left turn on to Waterloo Bridge.

This is its grandest moment, powering between breathtaking Thames views on both sides — the London Eye, the City, South Bank complex, Westminster. Then round the Imax cinema, which sits starkly in the middle of a roundabout; past Waterloo station on the right; and past the Old Vic theatre (once home to the National Theatre) on the left.

Then it presses on down Waterloo Road, past tall but indeterminate buildings towards Elephant and Castle. It's hard to get enthusiastic about the Elephant; it's really just a roundabout and one-way system, flanked by mostly undistinguished concrete buildings, including a shopping centre that seems to cry out for modernisation. The one surprising note is the neo-classical Metropolitan Tabernacle church, with a pillared portico like that of a Roman temple.

Catch a show at the Aldwych Theatre.

Then we're off down New Kent Road towards Bricklayers' Arms – which, contrary to its beguiling name, is not a pub (though it once was a coaching inn), but a busy road junction with a flyover taking A2 traffic on to the Old Kent Road.

We hive off left towards Tower Bridge, then quickly turn right along Grange Road and eastwards towards South Bermondsey, and here's a surprise: a shopping street consisting of low-rise 1960s buildings, a bit like a new town centre.

Another surprise for much of this part of the route is the speed humps, which make for a somewhat jolting ride. The Volvos' suspension simply wasn't designed to sop up something as hostile as this.

Then we make an unexpected turn north at Surrey Quays, where a busy shopping street forms part of the old town of Rotherhithe, and head towards Surrey Quays shopping centre; then we make our final right turn into Canada Water.

What a contrast. After the mixed but largely traditional landscape of our journey, we're into gleaming postmodern blocks of offices, flats and waterfront housing, and the glass and steel Canada Water bus and Underground station, with its circular entrance hall.

Immediately adjacent is Surrey Quays shopping centre, making the area even more of a magnet for visitors. It has its own bus station on the other side of the modest Canada Water basin, and this forms the 1's first call on the London-bound journey, though curiously it ignores this stop on the outbound trip.

So this is numero uno: an intriguing route, but perhaps not now delivering the full grandeur of the service in its heyday, when it crossed the whole of central London diagonally and penetrated much farther into the suburbs. ■ **PR**

Former hospital and part of the circular Imax theatre at Waterloo.

The Home Front

Six-wheel AEC Renown LT669, new in 1931, was caught in a bombing raid on Balham, south London in October 1940. Although its body was destroyed, the chassis was fitted with a spare replacement of different design and it remained in London Transport service until June 1949. This graphic image is among the displays at the London Bus Museum. GB

London Transport faced one of its toughest tests during World War 2, when garages and buses were destroyed, staff displayed heroism in the face of great danger and the materials shortages stretched resources to their limits

London Transport was well prepared for World War 2, which it had been convinced for some years was inevitable.

A huge number of employees was involved in these preparations and in carrying them out, but the inspiration for coping with everything that the Luftwaffe would throw at it and from which London Transport would emerge triumphant if battered was provided by Lord Ashfield and Frank Pick.

When prime minister Neville Chamberlain, in deep despair, announced on 3 September, 1939 to the House of Commons that we were at war with Nazi Germany, London Transport was already on the third day of a four-day evacuation to move 1,218,000 people, half of them schoolchildren and their teachers, out of London to safety in the country.

A fleet of 4,985 buses, 533 trams and 377 trolleybuses took them to

72 Underground stations and 129 'entraining main-line stations' in the suburbs to avoid too much congestion at the main-line termini.

Normal services were disrupted but they would have been anyhow, for on 23 September London Transport had its diesel and petrol allocation reduced by 25%. Many of the oldest, non-standard vehicles were taken out of service and in addition the majority of the ST class AEC Regents dating from 1930 were withdrawn.

These buses were doubly disadvantaged on account of having petrol engines, petrol being in greater demand than diesel, and only 48 seats compared with the 56 of most other standard double-deckers.

Ten years was at this time considered the normal life span of a London bus, so the STs were very nearly time-expired anyhow, but wartime conditions meant

that nearly all returned to service and did not finally leave the streets of London until 1950.

Trolleybuses keep coming

London Transport was halfway through the huge task of replacing all its trams by trolleybuses and for a while this continued, East London tram route 77 being replaced on 10 September 1939 by trolleybus route 677. Indeed trolleybuses, to full prewar specification, continued to join the fleet until October 1941.

On 5 November 1939 Bow Depot lost its trams, trolleybuses taking over its two routes, then on 10 November tram route 11 between Moorgate and Highgate Village, which had been worked by class HR2 (Hilly Route cars, was replaced by trolleybuses fitted with special coasting brakes to cope with the steep ascent of Highgate Hill. And finally, in June 1940 Poplar Depot said goodbye to its trams.

This left north London bereft of trams, except for three routes that passed through the Kingsway Tunnel, but the south London network was still largely intact and would remain so until 1950. Electrically powered vehicles became

A line of petrol-engined Renowns, headed by LT580 of 1931, parked on the Victoria Embankment in July 1942 between the peaks. By keeping hundreds on buses immobilised in central London during the day rather than run them back to their suburban garages with a handful of passengers, London Transport aimed to reduce the number of miles run by 2million and said that this speeded up other traffic in the Strand and across the West Eng. TOPICAL PRESS

An experimental producer gas installation on the back of a London Transport double-decker. The preferred method adopted in London and beyond was to tow the equipment on a small single-axle trailer. AEC

A mobile staff canteen for bus crews, apparently at Aldgate, in May 1942. The LT parked behind has anti-blast netting, the diamond patterns on both decks being the small area providing clearer outside visibility. LONDON TRANSPORT

of great strategic importance during the war, saving precious petrol and diesel, and some motorbus routes that paralleled tram or trolleybus routes or Underground lines were withdrawn.

The new standard London motorbus, the RT, was only just entering production when war broke out and it was not until January 1940 that the 150 production examples began to enter service from Chelverton Road, Putney on route 30, delivery continuing until January 1942.

The Green Line network was shut down on 31 August 1939 and in the remarkable short time of two days 477 of its vehicles were converted to ambulances. Later, when the United States entered the war, 55 Green Line coaches became 'Clubmobiles' for American troops, which provided them with comfort and entertainment. Almost all returned to Green Line service once the war was over.

Some routes returned in a modified form at the very end of 1939, often worked by double-deck buses, but by the summer of 1942 such was the strain on

the vehicles, maintenance being much reduced and petrol and diesel becoming ever more precious, that all Green Line services ended and would not resume until 1946.

Blackout and Blitz

Despite the expected bombs raining down on London within days of the declaration of war, the period known as the Phoney War ensued and a strange sort of twilight, neither war nor peace, descended upon the nation.

Blackout regulations meant that street lighting was much reduced, all vehicles had masked head and sidelights, and venturing out at night became fraught with danger. In the borough of Hackney, road deaths grew by 40% and this was fairly typical of London generally. Some people resorted to walking home along tramlines; others simply did not spot the sidelights of vehicles until it was too late.

Buses had their wing tips and platform edges painted white. In December 1940, three months after the first bombing raids, figures were released showing that 19,545 civilians had been killed by enemy action in London, while road deaths since September 1939 amounted to 11.434.

The Blitzkrieg — better known here as Blitz — began on 7 September 1940. It was still summer, skies were blue, the sun shone and the German bombers, based at captured French bases, came in over the Thames Estuary. A thousand bombers took part and they would return each day and night, using the Thames as a navigation aid, for the next 57 consecutive days.

The East End, the area around the busiest docks in the world, took the brunt and huge disruption was caused to bus, tram, trolleybus and Underground services. To quote Ken Blacker in his book, *London Buses and the Second World War,* 'The very act of taking a vehicle out on to the streets became one of heroism in itself.'

The West End and the western suburbs were virtually untouched and people clambered aboard buses to get away from the bombs. Another transport historian, Ken Glazier, wrote that 'the sight of the victims using public transport sometimes proved too much; unbelievably many complaints were made.'

The greatest damage to the fleet generally occurred at depots and garages at night. The first and, indeed greatest, loss to the tram fleet occurred on the night of 8 September 1940 when Camberwell Depot was hit and 29 cars were destroyed. Eleven were destroyed at Clapham depot a week later, and the depot was hit again on 16 April 1941. Six cars were destroyed at Abbey Wood depot on 7 November 1940, three at New Cross on 21 December.

Elsewhere bombs destroyed the tram tracks. Temporarily, trams terminated either side of the craters until the tracks could be restored, which was usually done remarkably quickly, the work quite often going on while bombs were still falling.

If trolleybus routes were disrupted and roads surfaces destroyed, the maintenance crews would erect temporary wiring along side roads.

Croydon bus garage received a direct hit on the night of 11 May 1941 and dozens of buses, all with petrol engines, were destroyed.

There would have been more had it not been for the bravery of Bill Maile. A driver at the garage, he heard the bombs fall at 02.55 and said to his wife, 'I must go round there. Four bombs had fallen, it was a raging furnace...I grabbed all the time cards...and then I thought, "The best thing to do is to save some buses".'

He got all the front line out safely, all the next row were on fire, so he went round the back and drove out more. Bill Maile, who lived to celebrate his 100th birthday in September 2004, was later commended for devotion to duty and awarded a £5 cheque. The next morning all Croydon Garage's services were operating, replacement buses having been brought in from elsewhere during the night.

At first, when the air raid sirens sounded drivers were told to evacuate

An STL, with masked headlamps and white-edged mudguards, negotiating a section of wooden temporary roadway following heavy bomb damage on part of route 19. FOX PHOTOS

their vehicles and take the passengers to the nearest shelter, but after a while they generally carried on unless the bombers were directly overhead. One said, 'I never believed in parking up a bus, as I considered it was in Mr Hitler's favour to do so.'

Many felt safer in a bus and especially in a solidly built tram, although this was an illusion and flying glass caused terrible injuries. To counteract this, anti-blast netting was stuck on windows, but passengers, frustrated by not being able to see where they were, tended to pick at the netting. Eventually a small diamond shaped area was left clear and this sufficed.

Replacement buses

At the height of the Blitz, Lord Ashfield appealed for help to cover the losses to enemy bombing. It has always been suspected that this was at least partly a propaganda measure to unite the provinces with the capital, for no more than 1% of the fleet had been lost and there were plenty of buses and trams in store.

Whatever, the response was immediate and before the end of 1940 the first of 475 buses began arriving from all over England, Wales and Scotland. Bournemouth even sent 18 trolleybuses, which worked in the Ilford area.

These 475 were something of a mixed blessing, for although the majority were AECs or Leylands with which London Transport engineers were familiar, there were also Crossleys, Albions, ancient ADCs and the like.

The last returned home — a few never did, having been damaged beyond repair — by February 1942, but before that London had returned the compliment by sending almost 300 STs to the provinces, beginning with Coventry which suffered dreadfully on one awful night in November 1940. Nearly half of these STs —146 of them —were the Thomas Tilling version with open staircases, many of which London Transport had already taken out of service before the outbreak of war but not broken up.

The reduction in supplies of diesel and petrol hit London Transport hard. Dependent upon supplies from abroad, the toll taken on the merchant shipping fleet in terms of both men and ships was horrendous although, as with London Transport, many were the heroic deeds by seamen in carrying out their duties.

One not particularly satisfactory substitute for petrol was producer gas.

Some STs and single-deck AEC Regals were attached to two-wheel trailers, which one writer described as most closely resembling a mobile hot chestnut cooker. These burned anthracite treated with sodium carbonate, which produced a gas, and after various processes this passed through a mixing valve into the engine.

They were prone to catching fire, not a particularly desirable attribute in wartime, and their efficiency was around 50% of the vehicles' normal output. But nine Regals and 172 STs gamely struggled on so equipped between the summer of 1942 and September 1944.

A drop in the ocean

Despite the initial reduction in services, such was the increasing demand for public transport, with all private motoring banned other than for essential purposes, that London Transport found it hard pressed to accommodate everyone.

The obvious solution was new vehicles, but where would they be built? The London Transport works at Chiswick went over to overhauling Rolls-Royce Merlin engines for Spitfires and in 1941 London Transport set up the London Aircraft Production Group and helped build 6,176 Halifax bombers.

It was a struggle to provide the most basic maintenance for the bus, tram and trolleybus fleet and in early 1941 the Ministry of Supply allowed work to be completed on bus chassis that had stopped (frozen) in September 1939.

London was allocated only 44 of these 'unfrozen' buses, 34 AEC Regents and 10 Leyland Titans, a mere drop in the ocean. Chiswick Works fitted some of the Regents with lowbridge bodies, which enabled them to take over routes previously worked by single-deckers. The quality of these bodies was poor, with single-skin roofs, much reduced opening windows, wooden-bodied seats and framework of unseasoned timber.

Clearly something on a much larger scale was necessary and in 1942 Guy Motors of Wolverhampton was given permission to start production of its double-deck Arab chassis with bodies from a variety of manufacturers. Later the Daimler factory, also in Wolverhampton, restarted and then Bristol was allowed to join in.

On all these the bodies, like those on the unfrozen AECs, were unavoidably way below the standards to which Londoners were accustomed, some even having wooden seats.

In all, London Transport received 435 Guy Arabs, 281 Daimlers and 29 Bristols, the last arriving in November 1946, 18months after the end of the war in Europe.

There also were 43 trolleybuses intended for South Africa — 25 Leylands, the rest AECs. War restrictions meant they could not be shipped and although they were 6in wider than the 7ft 6in that the Metropolitan Police allowed, this regulation was relaxed on the strict understanding that they were kept to the Ilford local services and never allowed to venture towards the City or West End.

By the end of the war 108 members of staff had been killed while on duty, 1,867 injured, 166 motorbuses and coaches destroyed, as were 17 trolleybuses plus 61 that lost their bodies but were fitted with new ones. Approximately 70 trams were destroyed and almost all the others knocked about and damaged to a greater or lesser degree. ■ MB

The 435 wartime Guys came in several forms. G171, photographed postwar in Dagenham, was among the later examples, delivered in July 1945 after the war in Europe had ended. It is an Arab II with Northern Counties body, one of 43 to see lengthy service in the British Transport Commission's Alexander fleet in Scotland following sale in 1951. F. G. REYNOLDS

THE STD

An unusual but significant order in 1937 — Coronation year — was for 100 Leyland Titan TD4 double-deckers, the STD class.

To the untrained eye, they might have looked remarkably similar to the standard AEC Regent-based STL, but Leyland built the all-metal bodywork at its main works in Lancashire. Leyland had borrowed the body of STL1217 to effect a suitable copy.

The chassis was largely Leyland's standard used widely outside London, but these 100 buses had AEC's worm and nut steering. Ninety had manual 'crash' gearboxes, but the other 10 had a Lysholm-Smith torque converter automatic transmission that Leyland had been supplying as an alternative to the preselector option available from AEC and Daimler. Leyland promoted this as its 'Gearless' solution.

There had been various improvements and innovations with successive batches of STLs but London Transport had become particularly interested in direct fuel injection as fitted to the STDs, and they showed almost a 1mpg improvement in fuel consumption compared to STLs. However, the noisy torque converter buses returned 0.7mpg worse fuel consumption than preselector STLs.

The Leyland engine, however, was

STD127, one of 22 of the 1946 PD1s allocated to Victoria, photographed when new in October 1946. LONDON TRANSPORT

quieter than the AEC and besides being more economical the engine was more reliable, as also were the brakes. This provided some of the pressure and technical knowledge for AEC to improve its products.

These 100 STDs spent most of their lives at Hendon garage, but moved around latterly still at garages north of the Thames. They were sold between 1953 and 1955.

Eleven 'unfrozen' Titan TD7 with Park Royal wartime utility bodies followed in 1941 and were allocated to Gillingham Street, Victoria garage. They ended their days as driver trainers, outlasting all of London's other wartime double-deckers, and were all sold by 1955.

The STD class was completed in 1946 with the first postwar peacetime buses for the Central Area, 65 Titan PD1s with Leyland's own bodywork. Beyond having roof number boxes, there was nothing particularly London about these buses, which met an urgent need for new vehicles. They had manual gearboxes.

They were shared between Victoria, Loughton, Hanwell and Croydon garages, though eight ran briefly at Potters Bar when new and some later operated at Leyton. They remained in service until service cuts in February 1955 rendered them redundant. All 65 were exported to Yugoslavia. ■ AM

STD38 from the batch of 100 Titan TD4s new in 1937. Although of the same outline shape as its standard product, their Leyland bodies incorporated many STL features. J. F. HIGHAM

MetroCity - for London

Optare customers have come to expect style, comfort and fuel economy from our vehicles and the new MetroCity is no exception. Our unique, fully integral stainless steel structure is once again the underlying foundation to provide the lowest design weight, and is already delivering class leading fuel efficiency in our Solo, Versa and Tempo models.

Progressive styling both inside and out, together with a comfortable, spacious interior are key ingredients to enhancing the travelling experience for passengers and encouraging more car owners to take the bus.

MetroCity is an evolution, not a revolution and draws on the reliability and durability of its award winning stablemates. It's available with diesel, hybrid or full electric drive in a choice of lengths at 9.9m and 10.6m, and with a total capacity of up to 60 passengers, this exceptional new model is sure to be a winner for our customers and a huge hit with operators, particularly in London.

Optare - good for the environment, good for the bottom line!

For more information, call the manufacturer of choice

08434 873200

or e-mail bussales@optare.com, www.optare.com

An ASHOK LEYLAND Company

Postwar
progress & problems

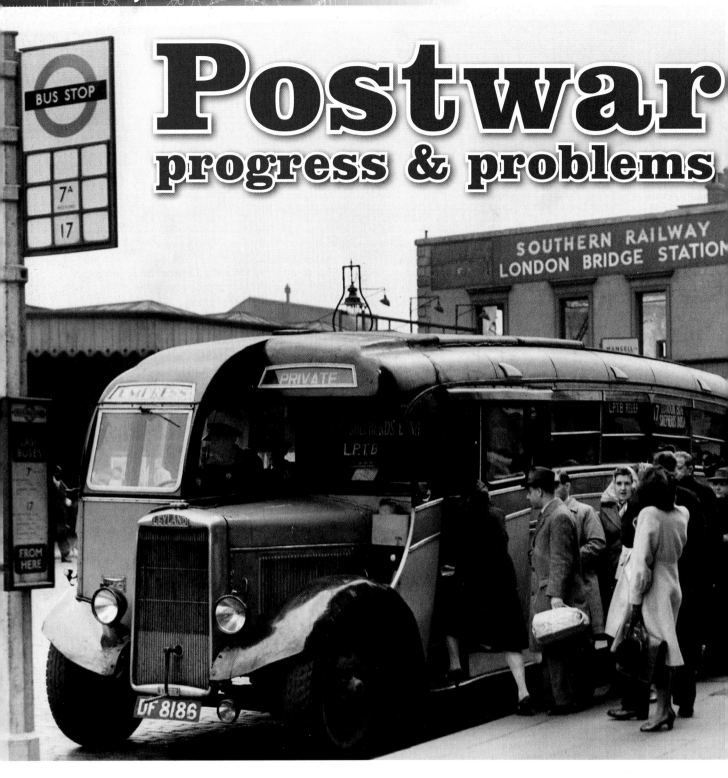

London Transport found itself at the end of World War 2 battered and bruised like the city it served but undefeated. There was a lot of catching up to do and there were changes of policy. The catching up included renewing and renovating a bus fleet that London Transport had been compelled to keep for a lot longer than the prewar average lifespan of around 10 years. Eager to revive production of the RT double-decker, it ordered 1,000 one year before the war ended, but materials shortages and a focus on exports meant that progress was slow.

Its needs were great. In 1948 there were still 1,139 ST double-deckers, 1,429 six-wheel LT double- and single-deckers and 429 AEC Regal single-deckers dating from 1929-33, all of which should have gone by 1943. The tram should also have disappeared by 1943 and by 1948 the oldest of these were 41 years old.

One of the changes of policy was to replace the remaining trams with motorbuses rather than trolleybuses. It was October 1950 when London saw the beginning of the end of its first generation of trams, replaced at roughly three-month intervals by around 800 mainly new

buses. On the night of 6/7 July 1952, huge crowds, most rejoicing modernisation but with a tinge of regret at the passing of an old, if somewhat enfeebled friend, saw the last car make its way into the scrapyard at Penhall Road, Charlton. Most of the newest trams were sold for a few years' further service in Leeds.

London Transport itself also changed. In 1933, it was one of few public boards in any sphere of British life, but the Labour government elected in 1945 was committed to bringing what it termed the commanding heights of the economy into public ownership, among them the

Thousands of new standardised buses arrive, trams and trolleybuses go but services are cut as people's lives change and they turn to other transport

Among the surplus buses sold to Ceylon Transport Board was Mann Egerton-bodied AEC Regal III T786. A Country Area green bus from delivery in 1948 to coming out of service in 1960, it operated from the Central Area garage at Norbiton, near Kingston in 1958 when this photograph was taken at Hampton Court. JIM THOMSON

Left: In October 1947, at the start o the loan of hundreds of coaches from private operators, passengers at London Bridge queue to file aboard a London Lorries-bodied Leyland Tiger TS2 of Empress Coaches. This operator was based in Hammersmith, from where the 32-seat coach is operating on route 17. FOX PHOTOS

railways, buses and road haulage.

It created the British Transport Commission to look after these newly nationalised interests from January 1948 and, after 15 years, the London Passenger Transport Board was brought into state control and reformed as the London Transport Executive, a division within the BTC. The government appointed Lord Latham, former leader of London County Council, as its chairman. Frank Pick had died in 1941; Lord Ashfield retired in 1947 and died the following year.

To the outside world and especially ordinary Londoners, it remained what

it had been from its formation: London Transport. But it was now an important part of a much bigger organisation.

In September 1951, BTC tidied up one of the awkward boundaries affecting bus services in the Country Area by transferring the Grays area routes of Eastern National to London Transport.

Before then, the BTC started to address London Transport's acute shortage of new buses. The last of the Bristol, Guy and Daimler utility double-deckers, to slightly relaxed specifications, continued arriving until November 1946. In late 1945, 20 postwar STL-class AEC Regents with Weymann bodies were delivered to the Country Area.

Shortly afterwards 65 Leyland Titan PD1s, like these STLs to provincial standards, were delivered to central London routes.

Also in 1946-48, two further varieties of front-engined AEC Regal single-decker arrived, continuing the T class that General originated in 1929, along with a new TD class of Leyland Tiger PS1s. The first 31 Tigers had standard provincial bodies by Weymann, identical to those on the first 50 postwar Ts, but the second 100 with Mann Egerton bodies built in Norwich were clearly designed by someone who knew what a London Transport single-decker should look like.

Again, these were identical to the final T bodies, except that the 50 Mann Egerton Ts, intended for the Country Area and painted green, had sliding doors. It took until May 1947 for the first

postwar RT to enter service and only 171 were in service by the end of 1947.

A lot more life needed to be squeezed out of prewar buses and between November 1945 and October 1949, 1,106 were sent off to outside contractors to have their bodies renovated and thus remain fit for a few more years' service.

Such was the lack of serviceable vehicles, however, that between October 1947 and August 1949 London Transport hired at least 945 coaches and single-deck buses from private operators, mainly for operation in the rush hours.

This was an expensive and complicated arrangement, and in late 1948 the BTC directed that 180 new Bristol double-deckers be allocated to London Transport for one year. These were painted in the green or red liveries of the BTC-owned Tilling companies in England and south-west Scotland to which they were eventually delivered after running in London. The number of Bristols loaned to London increased to 190. Many of them had lowbridge bodies, a layout far from ideal for central London routes.

New buses by the thousand

London's need for lowbridge buses was very limited, although there were height-restricted routes in both the Country and Central areas that needed more than a single-decker.

Although a lower version of the RT was under consideration, BTC rode to the rescue when 20 brand new standard provincial Weymann-bodied AEC Regents became available from the Midland

General fleet in the East Midlands. This formed the beginning of the RLH class in 1950 and London Transport ordered another 56 in 1952.

By then, RT deliveries were well in hand and the older, worn-out vehicles could finally be retired. So were the wartime utilities. Generally their chassis and the engines proved satisfactory but not the bodies and all were taken out of service by January 1954. Many were sold to other operators — some to BTC fleets in other parts of Britain — who rebuilt or, more often, replaced the bodies.

By March 1953 just 558 prewar and wartime buses remained on 36 routes. They included 270 STLs, 184 Daimlers, 97 STDs and seven Bristols. The STLs were to last the longest, until the end of June 1954 in the Central Area and 1 September in the Country Area.

One further impact that BTC ownership had was on who might build London Transport's buses. Bristol, building bus chassis, and bodybuilder Eastern Coach Works (better known as ECW) had been acquired in September 1948 along with the Tilling bus companies and to protect other vehicle manufacturers the legislation creating BTC forbade any of its subsidiaries from selling products to other organisations.

London Transport bought no Bristols of its own during the BTC era, but the Country Bus & Coach department took 100 bodies from ECW in the 1950s.

A temporary surplus

Work had begun on developing the Routemaster in 1947 and the first prototype appeared in 1954 with three more to follow, but by then the

Postwar restoration of Green Line routes saw some of the later utility Daimler double-deckers used when new on the busiest services between Aldgate and outer east London between 1946 and 1950. Duple-bodied D173, a CWA6 with AEC 7.7litre engine, works the 722 to Upminster, with L3 class MCW chassisless trolleybus 1469 of November 1939 turning alongside.

optimism that had driven so much of the immediate postwar investment was turning to pessimism as life became far more difficult for London Transport and public transport operators across Britain.

People were becoming more prosperous and with petrol rationing over and huge numbers of private cars taking to the roads, plus television watching keeping more people at home in the evenings, the number of customers requiring London Transport's services was in decline.

As early as 1953 a government commission reported that 'congestion is already becoming critical.' Two years later it was noted that 'of 38 Green Line coaches checked at Oxford Circus during the morning peak…none was early or

on time with nearly 50% running 10 or more minutes more late.'

Forecasting is an inexact science, formed by looking at how we have got to where we are and taking an informed step of where we will be tomorrow if all the trends continue. London Transport had made its forecasts on the reasonable assumption that more people, not fewer, would need its buses by the end of the 1950s, so when decline set in it had too many buses. The postwar shortages had turned into a surplus.

The postwar investment programme had brought over 7,500 new RT family double-deckers and RF single-deckers into the fleet, but in 1954 63 red RTLs and 81 green RTs were put in store, unused, the reds at a country garage and the greens at a red garage, only entering service in dribs and drabs until the final ones took up work in 1959.

Such was the effect of these changes that all the non-standard immediate postwar double- and single-deckers and early and non-standard postwar RTs could be retired. Even when the last unused ones took to the road in 1959, these RTs and RTLs simply replaced older members of the RT family, which were sold on and snapped up by eager operators at home and abroad.

The export of surplus buses was often part of consultancy services London Transport provided overseas and large numbers were shipped to Yugoslavia and Ceylon (now Sri Lanka).

Services were being cut to match the fall in demand and on 30 April 1958 a

An early postwar view at the Royal Forest Hotel in Chingford capturing the mix of double-deckers to be found in London Transport service. Nearest the camera is Park Royal-bodied utility Guy G214, then an STL, Northern Counties-bodied utility Guy G305, a new RT, then two six-wheel prewar LTs. They Guys were among 60 sold to Edinburgh Corporation in 1952, heavily rebuilt with new bodies and used to replace some of that city's trams. MB COLLECTION

Work to remove tram tracks from Streatham High Road while RT2527 passes on route 133 for Liverpool Street. The colourful tickets are from the last week of London Transport trams in July 1952. V. C. JONES

further 109 buses were removed from the daily schedules. A pay dispute had been simmering for some time and on 5 May crews began a strike that lasted almost seven weeks, ending on 20 June. Some bus crews left for other jobs and many passengers made permanent new travel arrangements. From carrying 21% of commuters before the strike, buses carried only 16% afterwards.

Even more cuts were needed — 20 Central Area routes were axed immediately, three garages closed and there were further reductions in the Country Area.

People were also being encouraged to relocate from London to six new towns that began taking shape in the Country Area from the mid-1950s — Crawley to the south of London, Harlow, Hatfield, Hemel Hempstead, Stevenage and Welwyn Garden City to the north.

New bus garages opened at Hatfield

and Stevenage in 1959, Harlow in 1963, but with their low-density housing and car-friendly traffic systems, these were places where it was far from easy to run an attractive bus service. The move of people to the new towns and beyond also added to London Transport's growing difficulty in recruiting and training drivers and conductors.

The trolleybuses go

Although there would be no more replacement of trams by trolleybuses, 127 new postwar trolleybuses, the Q1s, were put into service in 1948 and in 1952/53, allowing the withdrawal of the original 1931 trolleybuses and other worn out ones.

Supplied by British United Traction, a joint AEC/Leyland selling organisation, they were little different from the prewar trolleybus, other than being 6in wider and having fewer but bigger side windows.

They were used mainly in the Kingston area where it was anticipated they would remain for perhaps 10 years after all other trolleybuses had disappeared from London.   In the end, London Transport saved itself the trouble of keeping these trolleybuses for their full working lives, finding homes for most Q1s on various systems in Spain.

The announcement that motorbuses would replace trolleybuses had been made in the summer of 1954, though it was March 1959 before the first of 14 conversions — at Bexleyheath and Carshalton — took place. The final stage was in Kingston on 8/9 May 1962. Routemaster production was timed to provide the replacement motorbuses, although surplus RTs and RTLs were used for the first three conversions.

Aside from the Q1s, most trolleybuses were scrapped. A similar fate was about to fall upon the BTC. ■ **MB/AM**

The second prototype Routemaster, RM2 with Weymann body and Leyland running units, pulling away from the Queens Building at London Airport around 1958. JIM THOMSON

Two of the postwar Q1 class BUT six-wheel trolleybuses with Metro-Cammell bodies, both new in 1948. When most of the Q1s were sold to Spain in 1960, leading vehicle here 1789 went to Coruna and 1839 behind to Zaragoza. JIM THOMSON

THE RT

RT1 — or at least its body and original registration — survives at the London Bus Museum.

If you looked along Oxford Street in the 1950s or much of the 1960s, the only buses you would see would be those of the RT family. They set new standards for durability and reliability but when they were built nobody even dreamt that they might still be running in the late 1970s.

They were not designed from scratch, but followed on from the successful STL. The main mechanical differences were the air operation of gearbox and brakes and the use of a 9.6litre engine derated rather than a 7.7litre engine. They also had some London quirks, such as the absence of an air cleaner and shock absorbers.

They were a driver's bus too, with fully adjustable seat and exceptional visibility given by the low position of engine and bonnet. If you ride on a preserved one in London today, they are sprightly and manoeuvrable — more so than newer buses — the only downside being the absence of power steering.

RT1 appeared in 1939. The next 150, which went into service between 1940 and 1942, had timber-framed Chiswick-built bodies with a conventional chassis extension behind the rear wheels.

There were relatively few chassis

The RTs with Cravens and Saunders bodies

Of all the London RTs the Cravens-bodied ones stood out. Five instead of four windows on each side, a deeper cream band above the front upper deck windows and a more sloping rear were features easily spotted.

If their arrival was a surprise to many, their premature departure was even more so. There were just 120, the result of a realisation back in 1946 of impending problems keeping the existing fleet on the road, given delays in building the necessary jigs before production could begin at Park Royal and Weymann.

So London Transport placed advertisements inviting applicants

to supply 100 bodies for delivery in 1947. Follow-up circulars to 30 bodybuilders of standing brought just five attendees to a meeting in December 1946. AEC had indicated it could supply more RT chassis.

Just two bodybuilders emerged, Cravens Railway Carriage & Wagon Company of Sheffield, which was building bus bodies to fill a lull in railway orders, and Saunders Engineering & Shipyard of Beaumaris, Anglesey, a relative newcomer to bus bodies, offered 240 — later increased to 250. Later still Saunders was able to obtain a modest further small order for another 50.

Both agreed to commence

deliveries in 12 months' time; both took about double that to begin, but that was the pattern generally with materials and labour in short supply.

The first 27 Cravens went to the Country Area at Watford and Windsor while the rest were spread across the Central Area.

By the mid-1950s, London Transport had more buses than it needed. The different pillars, different window sizes and much else were going to be an impediment to the flow-line, factory-style overhaul system that had been set up at Aldenham.

The first red Cravens were withdrawn in June 1955, then

promptly reinstated to cover extra work from a rail strike. Some red ones moved to the Country Area stayed there, but 50 red ones had been withdrawn by the end of 1955.

Between March and May 1956, the Country Area repainted 23 red ones green, a waste but the final Cravens were withdrawn in October 1956. They were offered to the Tilling Group, which like London Transport was part of the British Transport Commission, but a modern bus with a large engine, preselector gearbox and a greater thirst was anathema to engineers there.

So 119 were sold to Bird's Commercial Motors of Stratford-on-

Preserved RTW185 restored to its original livery with reduced size destination blinds used when postwar materials were in short supply.

The first postwar RT to appear, RT 402, stands at Victoria observed by a London Transport official. Behind it are typical 1947 parts of the fleet — a wartime utility Guy on the 76 and an LT six-wheeler on the 29. JMA COLLECTION

changes on the postwar ones, though AEC had made some changes to the engine. But the chassis was now cut off behind the rear wheels, the platform and stairs being carried by the body structure as on RT1, which was metal-framed.

Jig-built bodies

During the war London Transport built aircraft and that experience led to the decision that the RT bodies should be jig-built, like the planes. The decision initially led to considerable delays, and disapproval in government departments and elsewhere. But it provided virtually complete interchange of parts and simplified maintenance, overhaul and repair.

When planning had reached an advanced stage, official permission to proceed had to be sought from the Ministry of Supply and the Ministry of War Transport. The MoS described the bus as having 'a modified wartime

specification for a standard body of metal construction'. Near the end of the war, it gave approval to bodybuilders Park Royal and Weymann to give a percentage of all their production to the RT. But it was the Ministry of War Transport that in January 1946 actually had to give permission for 500 bodies to be ordered — 250 from each.

The order for 1,000 chassis had been placed with AEC in April 1944, and it had promised to begin deliveries in December 1945. It actually completed the first in March 1946, ironically way ahead of the first bodies. Both builders began receiving chassis from March 1946 and soon ran out of space, London Transport having to store chassis at three different locations.

In 1947 AEC had to suspend chassis production for five months. It was in May that year that Weymann delivered the first bodied RT, followed later that month by the first Park Royal. By the time production ended in 1954 the two had

built 5,450 bodies and AEC had supplied 4,674 chassis.

The original plan had been to first replace 1,400 petrol-engined buses, followed by 1,000 diesel-engined LT six-wheelers. First to go were meant to be the 215 open-staircase buses. The plan was changed because many of the diesel buses had bodies in as bad condition as the petrols. In the end body condition dictated withdrawal – and the last open-staircase bus was not taken out of service until April 1949.

But London Transport did keep its promise to staff that the first RTs would replace the six-wheeled open-stair LTs at Leyton and Potters Bar. However, the vehicle position was so desperate that most of these Renowns were then spread around other garages.

But all those RTs were not going to be enough. Park Royal and Weymann would only be able to produce 2,800 new buses by the end of 1950. Add in 1,800 more

Cravens-bodied Country Area RT1406 at Croxley Green. F. G. REYNOLDS

A line of seven new Saunders-bodied RTs crossing the Menai Bridge on the first stage of their delivery run to London. SAUNDERS-ROE

Avon, which quickly sold all, 30 of them going to Dundee Corporation to help replace its last trams. The 120th had been damaged under a low bridge, so its body was scrapped and the body off RT19, in use as instruction vehicle 1037J fitted. That body was the original one from RT1, which now happily restored

and registered EYK 396, you can see today at the London Bus Museum.

In contrast, the Saunders bodies enjoyed a long and happy life in London. The company was establishing itself as a bus bodybuilder after war work on building watercraft and aircraft. As it was not modifying an existing

design, but developing a new one, it was able to incorporate most standard RT shapes and fittings, its biggest difference being in the more complex patented pillars, which made repairing after any major accident damage a more complex job.

It was not until 1967 that

withdrawal of Saunders RTs got under way, with the last just making it into 1969. The Saunders were about the last RTs in the fleet with the front roof-mounted route number box. Like the Cravens, all its bodies had that feature, whereas Park Royal and Weymann changed over in late 1948.

RT bodies under construction at the Park Royal coachworks in London. JMA COLLECTION

RTL672, a Leyland with Metro-Cammell body new in 1950. This bus survives in preservation.
OMNIBUS SOCIETY/PETER HENSON

buses that by then would be 12 to 14 years old, which had also been neglected in the war, plus 1,100 buses to replace trams, meant many more were needed.

After earlier talks Leyland agreed to provide 1,000 double-deck chassis, to be delivered at 300 a year from mid-1948. It also offered a further 500 chassis of 8ft width, which it would body in its own works to become the RTW class. The Ministry of Transport agreed to this total order in February 1947. Metro-Cammell had agreed to provide 1,000 bodies for the Leylands.

The Leyland chassis were its Titan PD2, but with frames modified to RT shape at the front and with fluid flywheel and gearbox supplied by AEC.

Red and green rivalry

Selecting garages to receive the new buses meant giving similar numbers to each of the four central bus areas, plus from 1948 the Country Area. Even so, the central bus people were not happy when after its first 150 bodies Weymann switched to green ones.

Another problem was that many garages could not take RTs until garage entrance doorways were raised, even though RTs were only 14ft 3½in high, lower than most provincial highbridge buses. At Palmers Green the whole roof had to be jacked up, inch by inch.

Like the first postwar RTs, the Leylands also arrived late. Apart from the very first, production did not get going until late 1948, and Park Royal then bodied them as it was running out of AEC chassis, and Metro-Cammell was not yet able to start building.

But once Metro-Cammell got going and Park Royal also continued bodying Leylands as well as RTs, then new buses flooded in, aided by deliveries from Cravens and Saunders.

But a new problem was looming:

instead of too few bodies it was too few chassis. That led to the ill-fated SRT programme of adapting STL chassis and fitting them with new RT bodies.

Thus aided by the SRTs, 1949 saw an incredible 1,592 new double-deckers delivered, an amazing improvement on 1948 when the total was 755. Just one month into 1950 saw another milestone reached when the last petrol-engined buses (STs and some LTs and STLs) and the last diesel-engined LTs ceased public service.

Most of the 450 Metro-Cammell Leylands had arrived by the end of 1950, as had all 500 RTWs, which used the extra 6in of width mainly on wider gangways, and by mounting each pair of seats a little farther out it was possible to use standard seats.

These buses stayed on outer suburban routes until 1951, but mid-1950 saw three inner London comprehensive tests with them. Most impressive was the first when for five days every bus using a narrow stretch of road in Notting Hill Gate was an RTW. That involved training drivers and then 306 RTWs were transferred into 12 garages working the eight routes for those days.

Two further lesser tests followed in Shaftesbury Avenue and Threadneedle Street. All were observed by the Metropolitan and City Police and others. No problems were encountered and before the year-end the first inner London route was changed over

Instructions issued to Country Area drivers in 1948 on how to handle the RT. JMA COLLECTION

permanently. Only routes also served by trams were banned.

There were further orders for RTL chassis, placed in dribs and drabs, to bring the total to 1,631, but the maximum in service at one time never exceeded 1,537.

Overseas tours

Something new and morale-boosting in 1950 was a European tour by four RTs publicising the forthcoming Festival of Britain, and these four buses and others were used on a highly successful innovation in 1951, service J, a tour of London by bus.

Over the next few years there were several overseas tours by London buses, the longest and most successful being by two RTs and one RTL to the United States and Canada in 1952.

The SRTs' bodies were remounted on new chassis and to hasten that process some RTs were reallocated to Chalk Farm. It was a Leyland garage, and mainly operated RTLs and RTWs. Adding RTs meant it became the only garage ever to run all four types at once.

March 1954 saw delivery of Park Royal-bodied RT4825, the very last, now preserved in the London Transport Museum.

Overhauling had begun well before then, building up to 56 buses a week on a three-year cycle. Quite soon that became a four-year cycle and docking intervals were stretched too as the bus proved surprisingly durable and reliable.

Metro-Cammell bodies were always kept on RTL chassis, and early RT bodies could

A typical West End scene full of RT family buses, with an RTL in front on the 25. BILL GODWIN

not be mounted on RTLs, but generally all were interchangeable. A few extra bodies had been bought to provide an overhaul float, but the system was fed by taking buses out of service for some time, during which both chassis and body would emerge with a new identity. An extreme case was RT497, which disappeared in December 1963 and did not reappear for over 14 years.

Overhaul intervals ultimately stretched to seven years — the length of a Certificate of Fitness — with an intermediate repaint at three-and-a-half years. The system meant that a long view had to be taken of future requirements. But calculations for the last RT overhauls proved wrong, and there was considerable slippage with many surviving RTs having to receive short-term recertification. RT4401, last overhauled in December 1963, survived until June 1978. RT overhauling finally ceased in 1970.

Bigger scale replacement
Once the trolleybuses went in May 1962, RT replacement began on a bigger scale. Initially the 1940-42 RTs used as driver trainers were replaced by RTLs. But soon RTLs started to be placed on the disposals list, as well as RTs carrying roof number box bodies.

The Leylands had never been as popular with drivers or maintenance staff, so their removal would simplify maintenance and spares holdings. Soon RTWs too began to be replaced by Routemasters, and their use as trainers was logical because of their width, the same as a Routemaster.

London Transport had only recently decided to fit heaters to its buses, and only to vehicles judged to have at least

an eight-year life expectancy. That would see off all Leylands, and all top box RTs, which also meant the end of Saunders-bodied ones. Some RTLs were still being overhauled but they were gaining roof-box bodies often older than the chassis.

RTWs had ceased to be overhauled after April 1962, and the last RTWs went off service in May 1966. The last RTLs were overhauled in January 1966, and the last went off service in November 1968. A new reason for replacing RTs came from 1966 onwards when falling traffic began to see some outer suburban routes replaced by one-man-operated single-deckers. The same year also saw a big drive to eliminate Metro-Cammell RTLs, with few surviving into 1967.

The final years
As new single-deckers were introduced in the Country Area, surplus green RTs were repainted red to speed the move to dispose of non-heater fitted red ones. The final roof-box RT, a Saunders one, was withdrawn in March 1971, leaving just Park Royal and Weymann-bodied buses in service, but these buses still had life in them.

Problems with new single-deckers and a lack of serviceable Routemasters led to a major programme of recertification in 1972 of RTs with Certificates of Fitness about to expire. Those in good structural condition went to Aldenham Works and after necessary repairs or replacements were repainted inside and out. Thirty-four others were bought back from London Country, the old Country Bus & Coach department, and repainted red.

Nearly 1,000 RTs were still licensed at the beginning of 1975, which had

The SRT rebuilds
The other oddities in the RT fleet were the ill-fated SRTs. This time round the forecast shortage was of chassis, not bodies, and London Transport desperately wanted to avoid having to ask Park Royal or Weymann to slow their deliveries, as they feared it might not then later be possible to increase them.

So a bizarre plan was drawn up to reconfigure the chassis of most of the last batches of pre-war STLs to take standard RT bodies: the good STL bodies off these would be used to replace earlier STL bodies.

From October 1948, the STL chassis were stripped and crossmembers and rivets removed, and their main frames heated to bend them to RT shape, after which new crossmembers were fitted in different locations, 7.7litre engine and auxiliaries refitted and standard RT steering and column mounted gearchange lever added. But the gearchange was not air-operated. Park Royal then bodied them.

The first went to Palmers Green for the busy route 34. But after much driver and union unhappiness, in a test an SRT was loaded with sandbags to simulate a full passenger load, driven down the 34 and the bell sounded for a request stop. The bus finally came to a standstill at the following stop.

Twickenham-based SRT159 with a 1950 Park Royal body fitted on the heavily rebuilt 1937 chassis of STL2405. The body went on to new RT4556 in 1954. JMA

Almost all SRTs were temporarily withdrawn and Palmers Green garage gained elderly STs and anything else that could be found quickly. The brakes were modified, and all SRTs were then put on quiet, flat routes, where they continued to be disliked by drivers — the 7.7litre engine was now propelling a bus more than half a ton heavier.

The buses still sounded like STLs and could also be distinguished by their FJJ and FXT registrations, with DGX and ELP among other letters distinguishing later SRTs rebuilt from older STLs. But the build was cut short at 160 instead of the intended 300. An extra order for RT chassis saw all withdrawn in 1953 and 1954, and bodies transferred to the new chassis. The final irony was that a handful of unadulterated STLs outlived them by a month or two.

Two Weymann-bodied RTs with roof number boxes to the fore in a busy scene in Windsor. Both were new in 1948. Country Area RT1000 is on the left, red RT498 on the right. OMNIBUS SOCIETY/ROY MARSHALL

once been a target date for the last to go. Another programme of three-year recertification began, this time at some garages as well as Aldenham. Another 65 were set for recertification in 1977.

London Country's last RT fell out of service in 1978 and London Transport intended that its last RT routes would be converted by October that year. Then crews at Barking, the last RT stronghold, said they would refuse to run Routemasters on route 62 because of the narrowness of Chadwell Heath station

bridge, so that one route remained into the New Year. By then it had just 13 RTs available for a scheduled need for 10.

Arrangements were made to divert the route away from that bridge, and with much ceremony Saturday 7 April 1979 was announced as the final day. The RTs were put out as normal on the Saturday morning, giving enthusiasts a last chance to ride on one and then, during the morning, Routemasters were substituted as crews became due for their meal relief.

Souvenir hunters over several days earlier had succeeded in removing the fleetnumber plate from the bonnet, but Barking garage had neatly applied gold transfers in the vacated place. The final journey was by RT624, nominally the oldest bus in the fleet. Then there was a gap until 16.00 when a 2hr long six-bus cavalcade left the garage. It was led by a police escort, which held up other traffic at junctions and was headed by restored RT1, with RT624 at the rear carrying dignitaries and invited guests. ■ **JMA**

Only a number, not any letters

Engineering staff at London's bus garages needed a comprehensive briefing about its new RT fleet, as so much was different to the STL. Until 1954, a purpose-built mobile training unit provided this. It was mounted on a new RT chassis carrying a converted double-deck bus body.

Converted is too mild a term, heavily and expensively adapted might be a better description. For the body, which retained its open staircase, had originally been mounted on a Tilling ST — and Tilling bodies were not noted for their strength. The RT had a longer wheelbase, a high driving position and a low-mounted engine. So considerable work and materials would have been needed.

Upstairs was a seated classroom, reached through a lockable doorway at the top of the stairs. The lower deck mainly comprised a floor with large trapdoors, which could be lifted to allow inspection of mechanical components. Examples of one or two smaller components were also displayed on shelves.

The bus visited garages in the weeks before they were due to receive their first RTs, so its presence was the first clue to enthusiasts of the likely next allocation of the type.

Use in this way of one of the oldest bodies in the fleet had an echo when the first RT went into service in 1938, as that carried the open-stair body off a

Leyland Titan originally owned by an independent. Perhaps the idea of a mix of oldest and newest appealed to somebody at Chiswick Works, where the adaptions were carried out.

The training unit never carried a proper number in the service fleet, just its chassis number — 0961079 — in gold transfers on its sides. In 1954 the body was scrapped and the chassis became RT4761.

Crystal Palace 3   Route 3

Route 3 passes many famous landmarks, starting with Oxford Circus at the north end and continuing right down to Crystal Palace in the south.

It has some rather nice buses, too — recent Alexander Dennis Enviro400Hs with a hybrid drivetrain. From the street they seem quieter than normal diesel buses, though when we rode on them the air conditioning was mostly blasting out at full tilt, drowning out our chance to hear what the engine sounded like on its own.

Abellio runs this route. It's a subsidiary of Nederlandse Spoorwegen, the Dutch state-owned train company, which has also become one of Britain's bigger train operators. After buying up Travel London, which previously ran National Express's bus operations in London, the group adopted the Abellio name — already used on buses in Germany — in the capital in

2009. It operates several hundred buses here.

The 3 is a north-south route, and starts in elegant style by heading down Regent Street to Piccadilly Circus. The white Victorian Lillywhites sports store on the south side forms a stylish backdrop to the Eros statue, these days no longer

The Crystal Palace transmission mast on Sydenham Hill, one of the highest points in London.

marooned on a roundabout, but still overlooked by the giant dot-matrix advertising hoarding on the corner of Shaftesbury Avenue.

Next we follow the one-way system into the Haymarket, a short but grand avenue flanked by theatres (on the way back the route uses Lower Regent Street, providing a similar experience). Then we enter the south side of Trafalgar Square via a narrow single-lane access into Cockspur Street — which is part of the A4, believe it or not.

Despite the Congestion Zone and repeated changes to the road layout, which have now blocked off the north and west sides of the square to traffic, this tiny chunk of journey can still take buses many minutes to complete; but if you're not in a hurry Trafalgar Square never fails to impress.

Nor does Whitehall, which usually seems unaccountably less crowded than other major thoroughfares in the area. The hubbub of the West End is largely absent here, as if hushed by the earnest if somewhat anonymous Victorian government buildings. Three of our six

Left: A hybrid Enviro400H at Brixton Underground station.

This page: Crowds in Trafalgar Square with St Martins-in-the-Fields and the base of Nelson's Column.

featured bus routes (the 3, 11 and 24) converge here on their way to and from Parliament Square at the south end.

Then the 3 does something unexpected. Eschewing Westminster Bridge, which beckons from the left just beyond Big Ben, it heads into Parliament Square and then straight on out of it past Westminster Hall, a mediaeval building that manages to blend unobtrusively into the Victorian Gothic Houses of Parliament. Then the 3 turns left on to Lambeth Bridge and past Lambeth Palace: the only double-decker route to cross the Thames here.

No tourists now, but a succession of broad tree-lined avenues fronted by Victorian town houses, flats and discreet office buildings. Lambeth Road takes us east to Kennington Road, where we turn southward and continue for a mile or two, skipping across to Kennington Park Road and then on into Brixton Road.

And abruptly we're in Brixton town centre, a thronging place of stores, street markets, pubs and multi-ethnic eateries. Here is the southern terminus of the Victoria Line, sporting what must surely be the biggest representation of the Underground roundel anywhere. Two railway bridges cross the main road at different heights at this point, towering

over the Marks & Spencer store and standing out unmistakably against the skyline.

On we go southwards, but just out of the town centre the 3 turns left off the main road into what looks like a suburban side street. It's Morval Road, part of a one-way system that takes us in a south-easterly direction towards Herne Hill.

It would be nice to report that Herne Hill is as pretty as its name suggests, but to bus travellers it's denoted chiefly by the Victorian railway viaduct that forms a backdrop to a tricky and often time-consuming right turn into Norwood Road. To our right all along here is Brockwell Park, but it's mostly higher than we are, so there's not a lot of it to see.

Then another of those unexpected left turns, taking us into the leafy lanes of West Dulwich: upmarket redbrick

Victorian terraced houses, pollarded lime trees, and (on our visit) a profusion of pink blossom.

On the horizon looms the television transmission mast at Crystal Palace, though we have a roundabout outside Gypsy Hill to negotiate first, then a curving tree-lined climb up to Crystal Palace Parade. In days gone by, buses terminating here would line up alongside Crystal Palace Park, but now they turn at a purpose-made bus station close to the town centre at Upper Norwood.

Sadly there's no Crystal Palace now. Built in Hyde Park in 1851 for the Great Exhibition, it was re-erected here three years later and survived until 1936, when it was burnt down. Even Crystal Palace football club is not actually here, but a mile or so away at Selhurst Park. But there's always that transmission mast. ■ **PR**

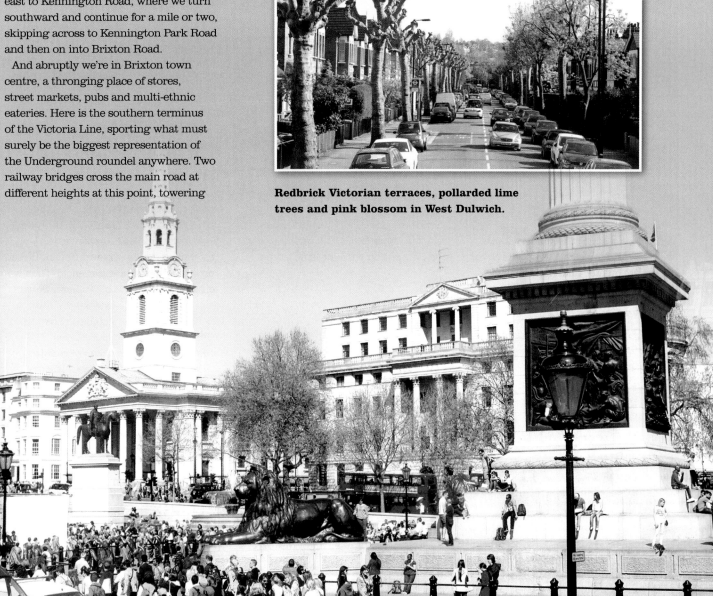

Redbrick Victorian terraces, pollarded lime trees and pink blossom in West Dulwich.

The RF & GS

Facing enormous problems just keeping its large and elderly fleet of double-deckers on the road, London Transport delayed renewing the smaller fleet of single-deckers.

Planning was complicated by the government indicating that it would raise the length limit for single-deckers from 27ft 6in to 30ft, but at an unspecified date. Width too presented a London problem. Outside London, 8ft was almost universal, but the Metropolitan Police still favoured 7ft 6in. Rather than go for a variety of lengths and widths, it opted for 7ft 6in for almost all its 715 underfloor-engined AEC Regal IVs, classed RF and RFW.

The new model had been announced in 1949 and London Transport had been running a demonstrator, UMP 227, for a considerable time. It needed new private hire coaches for the 1951 Festival of Britain, so ordered 25 in the shorter length; they were just about delivered in time. The remaining 675 were 30ft long.

The Regal IV had its underfloor engine mounted behind the driver on the offside, AEC having developed horizontal versions of the vertical 9.6litre engine powering the RT. There were air-operated brakes and gearbox, as on the RT. In many ways, the Regal IV was the logical development of the Q Type and lowering the engine was a significant achievement: RF coaches had all but one seat facing forwards.

One Q characteristic continued: the offside front spring contained more leaves to counter the higher weight on that side, and to partly balance that batteries and fuel tank were nearside mounted.

By a roundabout route the body contract went to Metro-Cammell, which had orders to build 1,000 double-deck bodies for RTLs, of which 400 were to be a version of its own design of metal-framed body, followed by the rest to standard RT style. Before the first were built, London Transport then asked Metro-Cammell what delay would be caused if all were RT style.

The bodybuilder reacted angrily, saying nine to 12 months and London Transport would have to pay for many components already built. London Transport then backed down, ultimately agreeing to the 400 as ordered, plus another 50, plus an order to body the 700 RFs.

The private hire coaches (RF1-25) were delivered in an attractive livery of traditional Lincoln green with flake grey top half. Fleetname and number were in red, not the usual gold. There were glazed quarterlights in the roof of these 25. There was a full-height half bulkhead behind the driver. A microphone, amplifier and loudspeaker were fitted.

Livery and indeed the appearance of all 700 RFs was the work of an external consultant, Douglas Scott, who later was involved with the Routemaster. He was particularly proud of the way the destination box blended into the front of the body, and of its square mudguards and bulls-eye (London Transport roundel) with filler cap behind.

Also delivered to the private hire fleet were five Eastern Coach Works-bodied 8ft wide RFW coaches to a design unique to them and to five more, also Regal IVs, for Tillings Transport, a British Transport

Private hire RF2 operated a London River Tour during the Festival of Britain. LONDON TRANSPORT

Commission coach company in London. They had glazed quarter lights, 39 luxury seats, a hinged entrance door and no destination boxes, as they were for longer-distance hires.

Delayed delivery

Problems at Metro-Cammell meant that the first 30ft Green Lines were delayed until late September. London Transport had planned for the first 37 prewar 10T10 coaches released from Green Line work to be modified for Central Buses, with heaters and ashtrays removed, linoleum floors replaced by wooden slats and other changes. Because the materials and works staff were ready, the work proceeded with the red buses then sent back to the Country Area, which reluctantly agreed to keep them off Green Line work.

The first 30ft RF began on Green Line 704 (Windsor-Tunbridge Wells) on 1 October 1951, with the last of the 263 Green Lines being delivered in October a

year later. They had air-operated folding platform doors and seated 39, all forward-facing except for a single, inward facing one behind the driver.

The parcels racks were integrated into the design of the interior with individual light bulbs (one for each pair of seats). Heaters were fitted and the seats had deep squabs: there were ashtrays on seat backs. Detractors called them Green Line buses, but their ambience was better than that of many 'proper' coaches. Compared to the sightseeing coaches, their wheelbase was longer, giving an extra window on each side and a longer overhang.

Externally they carried the usual wooden side route boards, and their Lincoln green livery was lightened by thin bands of a lighter green around the windows and front bull's eye. The Green Line RFs became the most reliable vehicles in the whole fleet, averaging 72,000 miles per failure or delay. But RFs were heavy, Green Line ones weighing

7ton 17cwt — 7cwt more than an RT.

Delivery of the 41-seat Central Area buses (RF289-513) followed directly, with a slight overlap. At the behest of the police they had no doors. Livery was red with cream bands, and black wings and lifeguards. There were inward facing seats (four on offside, five nearside) to provide extra circulation or standing space.

Other differences included wooden strip flooring and a bell cord running the length of the interior. There was no heating. They displaced mid-1930s 11T11s and the 9T9s of 1936 originally built as Green Lines but which were intensely disliked by Central Area drivers and conductors. Thus it was not until the end of January 1953, by which time over 125 Central RFs had entered service, that the last 1929 Ts and six-wheel LTs were withdrawn.

Final deliveries of RFs, this time Country Area buses, ran directly on after the Central ones. They had a folding door, while there was no metal-plate holder for a route number above the entrance. Deliveries were completed in December 1953. But three Country buses did not enter service until March 1954, appearing as full-sized one-man buses.

London Transport had looked at other operators with large buses that were worked by one man, and in particular at the Huddersfield Joint Omnibus Committee's 43-seat Guys. Having obtained dispensation for single-manning of buses seating more than 26, the three modified RFs went into service on an Epsom local route from March 1954.

The drivers' cabs were substantially modified and enclosed with a full height partly glazed door with a window containing slots for cash and tickets to be handed over. Mounted on the door were two Ultimate ticket machines and, to its left, a change-giving machine. The driver's offside windows were modified to provide an emergency exit.

Following trials also at Hemel Hempstead with a fourth bus, two returned permanently to the Epsom route from May 1955. The following year saw another 15 converted, and another 50 for 1957. As time went on, more and more Country Area buses were converted, the adaptions being simplified virtually every time. By early 1959 all Country RFs could be one-manned.

In the 1950s Green Line was growing and needed more vehicles. The first

An RFW on the London Airport Tour in the days when more people visited airports to watch other people using them than went there to catch flights.
GEOFFREY MORANT

Raincoats, hats, shopping baskets and a duffel bag are among the apparel and accoutrements of this group boarding Green Line RF312 operating a Country Area bus service in Reigate. GEOFFREY MORANT

step produced 40 more: 10 sightseeing coaches, six Central and 19 Country Area buses brought up — almost — to full Green Line specification. The sightseeing coaches lost their microphones and the six Central Area buses had doors added.

But there was fury among the Central busmen who had not been consulted about the loss of six vehicles. The last Country 10T10s having been retired in late 1954, the oldest buses were the early postwar Ts and TDs, nearly all of them in the Central Area.

The upshot was that Country Buses had, unwillingly, to pass six green ones to Central Buses to replace those purloined. A renumbering kept all the batches together, but after that when yet more bodies were modified the idea was dropped.

Further Country buses were borrowed to cover the first red overhauls. Surprisingly bodies needed to be modified at the first overhaul to simplify removal and refitting to suit the Aldenham flow-line system. The sightseeing batch never changed bodies but others did.

Central one-man operation

Having converted the last country buses for one-manning, work began in 1959 on the Central Area ones, which gained doors. But the one-man agreement in Central Buses had been terminated in 1949 when the last Leyland Cub 20-seaters at Romford were replaced. The union insisted on a much bigger premium for one-manning, so it was not until late 1964 that the first routes could

be introduced, following acceptance of the Phelps-Brown investigation and report into pay and conditions.at London Transport.

By this time Green Line requirements had been eased by converting scheduled weekday peak-hour duplicates to RTs, and in 1962 by the appearance of the first Routemaster Green Lines. Shortages of staff in the 1960s resulted in the decision to drop private hire work. By the end of 1964 all 25 sightseeing RFs and the 15 RFWs had been sold, 10 of the RFWs joining other surplus London buses in Ceylon.

By 1965 Green Line was in decline and 31 RFs were downgraded to 37-seat one-man buses. If it had been in better financial shape, London Transport might have replaced the RF coaches by then, but a realisation that they would have to remain prompted the experimental upgrade of one under the direction of designer Misha Black, better known in transport circles for his work for the new Victoria tube line.

In 1966 RF136 gained a curved windscreen on the driver's side, twin headlamps, curved mudguards and a deep light green band beneath the windows. Inside fluorescent lights were fitted and grey was used for side lining panels. The work was judged a great success and 174 more were modernised.

This is all the more remarkable when it is remembered that the vehicles had each already covered over 1 million miles. All were soon converted for one-man operation.

By 1968, Country Area service levels were being cut, RFs sometimes

replacing double-deckers; 24 refurbished RF Green Lines were downgraded to buses with a broad cream band replacing the light green. Following delivery of new Merlins, 13 Country RFs transferred to Central Buses in 1969.

When the Country Area transferred to the National Bus Company's London Country Bus Services in January 1970, 413 RFs went with it, only 37 fewer than were there in 1953. It also had on loan five red RFs, the last of which returned to London Transport in March 1971. They survived in ever diminishing numbers until the last of all, RF202, was retired in July 1979.

After the 1970 split, there still were 192 Central Area RFs, 64 crew operated and 128 one-man, a further 42 having been one-man RFs converted in 1966. In 1970, another 30 were converted for one-man operation, their entrance doors differing in having a single deep window on each leaf. Many went to Uxbridge in January 1971 to replace double-deckers on four routes. But 40 unconverted ones were withdrawn soon after.

More, then due a fourth overhaul, were withdrawn in 1973, with the aim of replacing the last in 1975/76. The plan was then for a few RF routes to go over to double-deckers or higher capacity single-deckers, but the layout of Kingston garage made this impossible for two routes and there we not enough new smaller single-deckers.

More RFs went in 1976, but to keep them going Hanwell and Stonebridge garages reconditioned 25 others to

GS35 in Windsor.
GEOFFREY MORANT

The Guy Specials

Last of all the prewar types to come up on London Transport's replacement plans were the 20-seat bonneted Leyland Cubs new in 1935/36, of which 55 were scheduled for daily use, mainly in small numbers from several Country Area garages.

There had been plans (including drawings by ECW) to rebody many, but Leyland then announced impending withdrawal of spares parts availability. With no suitable chassis available, Guy developed

When new, the Central Area RFs had an open front entrance and displayed the route number on a plate above the doorway. This is RF289. LONDON TRANSPORT

gain new three-year Certificates of Fitness. They continued running until someone solved the Kingston problem by moving the two routes to nearby Norbiton garage.

Their last day was 30 March 1979 with 17 buses in service, RF507 restored to 1953 livery being the last scheduled bus back at the garage, duplicated by two more RFs. The next day was a mayoral ceremony and three runs over both routes by other RFs for invited guests, with RF512 last back this time. Just a week after that, the last RT ran. ■ JMA

Preserved RF28 was one of 125 Green Line examples modernised in 1966/67 when it was already 16 years old.

a mix of its Vixen and Otter goods chassis, hence the class code GS — Guy Special.

The front end used the pressing built by Briggs Motor Bodies for normal control Ford Thames goods chassis and a Perkins P6 diesel engine and crash gearbox were fitted. The ECW body was designed to be similar in appearance to the RF, but had sliding top windows.

The 84 ordered were intended to cover 55 scheduled 'small saloon' workings plus spares, with a further 12 required to replace some 'large saloon' (RF or 10T10) workings. Dispensation was obtained for them to seat 26, instead of the normal legal limit of 20.

For a few years they worked as intended. But a slightly different use was on an hourly service between Dartford and Grays through the new

Dartford Tunnel. When it opened in 1963, London Transport extended a Green Line route through plus an RT double-deck service. Few people in Essex wanted to visit Kent, or vice-versa and those facilities vanished in less than a year, replaced by the hourly GS service.

Driving a sparsely laden bus at maximum revs 'on the governor' threw up a problem not previously faced: steering column fracture caused by vibration. An extra spare bus was then added to the Grays garage allocation, but the service was soon withdrawn.

Demand for GSs dropped fairly steadily through the 1960s, from 57 scheduled at the end of 1961 to 35 a year later, and then steadily down to three when London Country took over.

The Indian's head motif on the bonnets of all the GSs.

Last route of all was the 336A, until 1971 worked by a driver who lived on the Loudwater Estate, the route served by the bus. The bus was outstationed, and went to Garston garage on Friday mornings for the driver to pay the takings and collect his wages, and for the bus to be

refuelled and cleaned, or substituted by another GS.

When he retired the bus ran out from the garage each day, which ruined its operating costs. The last run in March 1972 was duplicated to cater for the enthusiasts and locals marking the occasion. ■ JMA

Route

If there is one bus that has caught the wider public's imagination, it is the London Transport Routemaster — to the extent that any double-decker with its engine at the front and an entrance at the rear is automatically dubbed a Routemaster, even when it is not.

From the late 1940s London Transport engineers had been looking to the next generation of London double-deckers and in 1947 it was given authority to develop a chassisless double-decker of aluminium construction. It worked with two of its principal suppliers, AEC and Park Royal, to design a bus that was light and strong, offering maximum passenger capacity and good performance.

Standardisation was important and mass production on a jig-built basis was the goal. London had experience of chassisless construction with MCW-built trolleybuses dating from 1939/40 but aluminium construction was still relatively new to the bus industry.

Although in its early stages the new bus might even have been designed as a trolleybus, it eventually materialised as a diesel bus that would replace London's large trolleybus fleet between 1959 and 1962.

The Routemaster, 'London's Bus of the Future', was first seen by the public at the 1954 Commercial Motor Show at London's Earls Court. At first glance it was not greatly different from its illustrious predecessor, the RT. The engine was at the front, the entrance at the rear, and while at 27ft 6in (8.2m) long by 8ft (2.4m) wide it was wider and longer than the standard RT it was a very different bus under its aluminium skin.

Gone was a heavy chassis, and in its place two sub-frames on which were mounted the main mechanical units and which supported the chassisless body.

Under the bonnet was an AEC A204 engine, largely the same as fitted to the RT type but the gearbox and brakes were hydraulically operated, a new departure. The epicyclic gearbox was directly operated with no gearchange pedal as on the RT family's preselector box.

The 64-seat body offered 14% more seats than an RT and came close to the 70 on longer six-wheel trolleybuses, while the aluminium construction allowed the unladen weight to reduce by more than a ton on the prototype and half a ton on production vehicles.

The most obvious new feature was the front end; in place of the exposed radiators of the RT family the Routemaster had a full-width front, and in the case of the prototype the radiator was actually under the floor, allowing a design that did not require a grille for a front-mounted radiator and allowed a simple design incorporating the LT roundel and some vertical chrome spikes. There was controversy over the greatly reduced front, side and rear destination displays, which came as a shock to many after the very informative displays of

RMF1254, the forward entrance Routemaster never operated in London Transport service, on the manufacturer's stand at Earls Court in 1962. LONDON TRANSPORT

the RTs but when the prototype entered service the Routemaster had more comprehensive destination displays.

RM1, the first Routemaster, went into service from Cricklewood garage on 8 February 1956 on route 2 (Golders Green-Crystal Palace). Production Routemasters would not enter service until three years later, so there was time to find out how well the new design performed.

It returned to Chiswick Works where a new AV600 engine of similar capacity was fitted and, as the law no longer restricted its length to 27ft, the radiator was moved to the conventional position ahead of the engine, behind a wider grille. It went back into service at Cricklewood in March 1957 but became a driver trainer in 1959 and never operated again in normal passenger service. It forms part of the London Transport Museum's reserve collection.

Three other prototypes followed. RM2 was ready in March 1955 and ran unpainted on various testing grounds. It initially had a 7.7litre AV470 engine but despite the lower weight of the Routemaster this left it underpowered and it had this replaced by a 9.6litre.

It was painted green for Country Area trials, undertaken alongside RTs between

Country Area RML2440 is preserved in its original Lincoln green and cream. AM

master

RM459 and RM954 passing each other on the A24 in North Cheam in August 1982 shortly before one-person-operated Fleetlines replaced Routemasters on route 93 from Putney Bridge. AM

May and August 1957 on route 406 between Reigate and Kingston. Then repainted red, it went to Turnham Green garage (conveniently close to Chiswick Works) for trials mainly on route 91 between December 1957 and November 1959, after which it too disappeared from passenger service. It awaits restoration to Country Area green, with a replica of its original grille and bonnet, at the London Transport Museum's Acton Depot annex.

The third red prototype was RML3 (plain RM3 from 1961), with Leyland O.600 engine and running units in a Weymann body. It was delivered in July

1957 and entered service from Willesden garage on routes 8 and 8B in January 1958 and joined the other prototypes as a driver trainer in November 1959. Restored to original condition in time for the Routemaster's 50th anniversary in 2004, it is part of the London Bus Museum collection.

Delivered ahead of RML3, in June 1957, was CRL4 (RMC4 from 1961), the prototype Green Line Routemaster. This also had Leyland running units, but in a body by state-owned Eastern Coach Works. It led a more active and public life than the other three, entering service at

Romford in October 1957 and remaining in service at various Country Area and London Country garages until 1979. London Country and successors retained it as a heritage vehicle before selling it for private preservation in 2006.

Three underframes disguised with slave rig lorry-style bodies had been pounding up and down the London streets since August 1958. Nominally, these were numbered RM5, 6 and 7.

Which left RM8 as the first production Routemaster to appear, at the September 1958 Commercial Motor Show when Leyland's futuristic rear-engined

Atlantean stole the limelight. This would become perhaps the most elusive of all Routemasters, as it was used to test out all sorts of clever ideas at Chiswick Works for the next 18 years before finally entering passenger service at Sidcup garage in March 1976. It was sold for preservation in 1985. It might never have even had those nine years at Sidcup had RM1368 not had its top deck destroyed by fire, leading to its conversion into a single-deck test bus.

After five months' trials at eight garages, either as trainers or alongside RT family on a variety of routes, the first 74 production Routemasters replaced trolleybuses at Poplar and West Ham on 11 November 1959. There were many teething problems with them, which took time to resolve, but the Routemaster was an integral part of the replacement of the rest of London's trolleybuses over the next two-and-a-half years.

Broadly similar

Production Routemasters were broadly similar to the prototypes but had new front-end structures to accommodate the front-mounted radiator and had full destination displays. All subsequent buses were built in London by AEC and Park Royal, although not all received the AEC AV590 engine as more than one-quarter of the production Routemasters (coded RM, the most numerous type) had Leyland O.600 units and others had AEC's bigger AV690.

Deliveries of the 2,120 8.4m-long RM-type Routemasters continued until 1965 but for a vehicle conceived as a highly standardised bus there was a remarkable number of variations.

First there was the RML, 30ft (9.1m) long with seats for 72 passengers. Two-axle buses to this length were not legal when the Routemaster was first conceived but from 1956 they were, so London Transport bought 24 RMLs in 1961 and its last 500 were also longer buses. One hundred of these went to the Country Area, painted green; in 1970 they passed with these operations to the new London Country company, but most later returned to London Transport.

Next there was the RMF, a 30ft Routemaster with a 69-seat forward entrance body, which was displayed at the 1962 Commercial Motor Show. It fell foul of trades union objections to its possible use without a conductor and never ran

in normal London Transport service but was sampled by three other operators, including British European Airways (BEA) for its service to London Airport.

In 1966 it was sold to Northern General Transport in north-east England where it joined 50 similar but in some ways mechanically different buses; these were the only new Routemasters built for an operator outside London and although 12 of these were bought by London Transport in 1979/80 they were sold or scrapped.

The Green Line network of limited stop services had been worked for many years by single-deck RFs, and although one of the four prototype Routemasters (Leyland/ECW-built CRL4, later RMC4) was a Green Line coach, no more were bought until 1962 when 68 RMCs were delivered with 57 coach seats, luggage racks and platform doors.

RTs already operated on busier Green Line routes through the East End, but the idea with the Routemasters was to use them to maintain capacity while reducing frequencies. For example, when they replaced RFs on the 715 between Guildford and Harlow the frequency came down from three to two an hour and on

Left: A 1956 photograph in Vauxhall Bridge Road, Victoria of RM1 in original condition. That year, the length limit for two-axle double-deckers was increased from 27ft to 30ft, allowing the radiator to be moved from under the floor to in front of the engine, replacing this original front and London Transport roundel with a more conventional grille. GEOFFREY MORANT

Right: RM8, the first production Routemaster that saw little passenger service, has been restored to the condition in which it appeared in 1958. AM

Below far left: Routemasters at Victoria shortly after the Victoria Line opened in September 1968. RM540 has the original radiator design with London Transport roundel above the grille, while RM2182 has the triangular AEC-style badge introduced in 1962 and ultimately applied to all buses. The BOAC advertisement above them offers 16 days in New York for £132. OMNIBUS SOCIETY/ROY MARSHALL

Left: Green Line RMC1461, in original livery without any commercial advertising on the sides, is part of the London Bus Museum collection. AM

the 720 between Bishop's Stortford and Aldgate it fell from half-hourly to hourly.

More Green Line Routemasters followed in 1965, 43 RCL types, 30ft long with seats for 65, replacing the RTs on the routes connecting Brentwood, Upminster and Tilbury with Aldgate.

Most of the RMCs and RCLs eventually returned to London Transport from London Country and while some RCLs were used in service, the RMCs became driver trainers.

BEA bought 65 forward-entrance 27ft 6in Routemasters in 1966, 56-seaters for the service linking the Gloucester Road air terminal and Heathrow, and these had towing bars for luggage trailers. They were geared to operate at 70mph on the M4. In 1975, LT bought 13 of these buses that were surplus to the airline's requirements, and, as RMAs they were placed very briefly in service.

Gradually the rest of the former BEA Routemasters found their way to London Transport, some for use as driver trainers, others mainly as staff buses shuttling employees from all over Greater London to and from Aldenham Works.

The most fundamental variation on the Routemaster theme was FRM1, the

solitary rear-engined example that was unveiled in 1966 and which is described on p62.

Production of the Routemaster ended with the arrival of RML2760 in February 1968. It operated first from Upton Park garage that month.

Many liveries
During their long lives Routemasters carried many liveries. Most wore variations of London Transport's red with various fleetnames and logos, both in London Transport days and then later when London Buses was restructured into 11 operating units, and into privatisation when some more distinctive liveries appeared, mostly respecting London red and the classic lines of the bus.

Two operators that won London contracts and adopted different colours were BTS, with poppy red Routemasters, and Kentish Bus with pale yellow and maroon ones. Later Routemasters, like the refurbished examples for route 19, ran in all-over red.

The RMLs for the LT Country Area were green, as were the RMC and RCL Routemaster coaches, and these later carried NBC leaf green under London

Country ownership.

RM664 operated from new in 1961 until 1965 in an unpainted 'silver' livery with red wheels and gold fleetnames. The idea had been tried in a few places in the 1950s to save weight and was adopted by London Transport on Underground trains. While RM664 was unique, special short-term liveries used by London Transport included the 25 silver SRMs for the Queen's silver jubilee in 1977.

They were followed by 12 green-painted examples marking the 150th anniversary of the first Shillibeer horse bus, in 1979. RM2 was painted in both of these liveries to demonstrate the opportunity to potential commercial advertisers. Other specials included the 16 red and yellow Shop Linker buses for a short-lived circular service in the West End; RM1983 among the gold buses marking London Transport's golden jubilee in 1983; and various retro liveries, recalling earlier London styles.

These were all highly restrained by comparison with the sometimes garish advertising liveries carried by 28 Routemasters at various points between August 1969 and May 1976.

The first significant withdrawals of

Routemasters started in 1982, following service reductions, with the intention of ending the employment of conductors. There was talk for a time of selling most of them to China, but instead their departure from London coincided with the deregulation of bus services in the rest of Britain and surplus Routemasters were a popular tool for operators looking for a quick, reliable double-decker that could beat its competitors away from bus stops. Glasgow, Carlisle, Blackpool, Manchester, Bedford and Southampton were among places that would enjoy Routemaster services between 1986 and the early 1990s.

Although the London fleet would be reduced over the next 20 years these buses still had plenty of life in them. They had seen off newer generations of double-decker and would enjoy a renaissance in their later years, confined to the busiest routes serving the heart of London.

The 1986 closure of Aldenham Works meant that regular and thorough overhauls of the type carried out there became more difficult. The answer was a major programme to bring the rather tired-looking RMLs up to standard and in 1992-94 most received an interior makeover involving new moquette and interior trim, new flooring and the installation of fluorescent lighting. Most also received new Cummins or Iveco engines with others later receiving Scania units.

One of the more ambitious exercises was undertaken by London Coaches, the sightseeing operation set up by London Buses in 1986. One of the features of open-top sightseeing buses is that most tourists want to sit upstairs regardless of the weather, so the more seats they have upstairs the better.

While a 30ft RML has 40 seats upstairs, London Coaches increased the earning potential of 10 standard RMs by taking

RM686 in Trafalgar Square, displaying the Vernon's Pools advertising livery it wore for two years from August 1972. OMNIBUS SOCIETY/ROY MARSHALL

a section out of scrap RMs to create a 31ft 6in long vehicle called the ERM with 44 seats upstairs (76 in total) instead of 36. This was another of the advantages of jig-built construction, though one that was probably never considered when London Transport engineers were designing the Routemaster more than 60 years ago.

After their retirement from London, the ERMs were sold to Lothian Buses for sightseeing services in Edinburgh.

Final years

Following the election of Mayor Ken Livingstone, Transport for London bought back 49 RMs from various sources and had these thoroughly refurbished, initially by Marshall's of Cambridge where they were repanelled and painted, given new internal and external electrics, and fitted with Cummins engines and Allison gearboxes.

But on re-election in 2004 Livingstone — who had said in 2001 that 'only some

Kentish Bus RML2505 in the variation of the operator's own livery applied to the buses operated on route 19. Kentish Bus — previously London Country South East — leased these buses from London Transport as part of the contract. AM

sort of ghastly dehumanised moron would want to get rid of Routemasters' — announced that they would be phased out to provide the UK capital with a totally accessible bus service. There were those who argued for the Routemaster, pointing to the ease and speed of boarding, and those who argued against it, suggesting that the lack of proper accessibility and the dangers of the open rear platform were reasons for its withdrawal.

The last Routemasters ran in normal London service with Arriva on route 159 in December 2005, with RM2217 — the highest numbered 64-seater — the last to depart Marble Arch for Streatham. Its later life was typical of this legendary type. An Iveco replaced its original engine in 1991 and from 1994 to 1998 it wore a red and cream livery unique to route 159. In 2001 it was fitted with a Cummins engine, Allison gearbox and Voith retarder.

In November 2005 new heritage services kept smartly refurbished examples on two tourist-focused central London routes (see p112). Then in 2008 new Mayor Boris Johnson pledged to introduce what he called a 'new Routemaster', which duly appeared in 2011 as the New Bus For London (see p118).

In June 2013 BBC Two began airing a documentary series about the role that Transport for London plays in keeping the roads flowing for the benefit of all traffic. And the name of this television programme? The Route Masters. After nearly 60 years, that classic double-decker has imprinted its name on the national psyche. ■ **GB**

A First London RML mops up a
queue at Paddington, May 2003. GB

Chiswick & Aldenham

Two massive central works used production line systems to overhaul and rebuild London Transport's highly standardised fleet

The imposing presence of Aldenham Works. AM

S upporting and in one case for a time building London's buses for many years were its two central works facilities at Chiswick and Aldenham.

Chiswick Works dated back to 1921 while Aldenham — near Elstree in Hertfordshire — became involved in bus work immediately after World War 2 and was fully functional from January 1956.

Until 1921, the London General Omnibus Company had its vehicles overhauled at a variety of establishments, including the home garage of each bus, which attended to the chassis. It made sense to combine everything on one site, so 32acres were bought immediately north of the Chiswick High Road.

Almost all General buses were of AEC manufacture and it must have been more than a coincidence that a few years later AEC moved from its original factory in Walthamstow to one at Southall, just down the road from Chiswick. In 1921 Chiswick was on the edge of suburbia, so land was relatively cheap.

This was just three years after the end of World War 1 and although the returning, surviving soldiers were supposed to find themselves welcomed back to a 'Land Fit for Heroes', many were unemployed. The government therefore provided some of the £5.5million needed to set up the Central Overhaul Depot, to give Chiswick its official title; 3,000 men and women were employed there. The canteen, which also served as a dance hall and was used for a variety of social activities, could seat 1,300.

Chiswick rapidly became the benchmark upon which other large transport organisations judged their own facilities. Each bus was overhauled once a year and so thorough was this work that when it emerged it was to all intents and purposes a new vehicle.

Through the 1920s and 1930s Chiswick not only overhauled all the General and London Transport buses and coaches — trams and trolleybuses were dealt with elsewhere — but also built most of the bodies and was constantly looking at ways of improving bus technology.

Jack Lemmer, who qualified as a unit adjuster (fitter) at Chiswick in 1927, and during the World War 2 was a leading light in introducing gas powered buses in order to save precious imported petrol and diesel, when interviewed at the age of 99 nearly 80 years later commented that the works 'simply buzzed with innovative ideas, clever dedicated men constantly seeking improvements in every aspect of bus design'.

Working closely with AEC and Leyland, Chiswick engineers in the 1930s helped develop the STL, STD and RT double-deckers as well as the pioneering rear- and underfloor-engined single-deckers, and postwar they played a major part in the Routemaster programme.

One of the most impressive features at Aldenham was the high bay where bodies were moved by overhead crane. Below the raised body of the RT with BOAC advertising is one of the inverters on which the underside of the body was sprayed with protective paint. Nearest the camera is an RT over one of the remount pits. JMA COLLECTION

The wonders of Aldenham

It had been intended that Aldenham would be the depot for a Northern tube line extension, which was begun in the 1930s but on the outbreak of war in 1939 it became part of London Aircraft Production, set up by London Transport and others to build Halifax bombers.

The extension was never completed, and with Chiswick struggling to cope with the huge backlog of work resulting from the six years of wartime neglect of the fleet, it was decided

that Aldenham would be ideal for overhauling bus bodies and chassis. By January 1956, it took over the overhaul of all London Transport buses from Chiswick, which then concentrated on running units like engines, gearboxes and axles.

There were 1,800 people at Aldenham, where overhauling a bus or coach was a highly sophisticated and fascinating process. The general public caught a glimpse of this in Cliff Richard's most successful film, *Summer Holiday* of 1962. He and his friends, The Shadows

and others, play the part of mechanics at Aldenham and decide to take an RT on a holiday to sunny southern Europe.

Filmed during the works summer shutdown, employees were used as extras and we are shown how the bus body was rotated so that it could be steam cleaned, then lifted high above the shop floor by travelling crane and placed where every part could be examined and made good.

The bus emerging from this process was seldom the same one that went in. When, let us say RT1138, was brought in early in the morning, it would appear to emerge sparkling and in tip-top mechanical condition later that afternoon. It still bore the fleetnumber RT1138 and its original registration plate, but that was all that linked it with the vehicle of a few hours earlier, for by then that would be in the process of having its body removed from its chassis, its component parts stripped, ready for either refurbishment or replacement.

The reason for this was to make full use of licences, for with a fleet of many thousand vehicles each day RT1138 and it companions spent idle cost London Transport thousands of pounds.

The bus that had gone in for overhaul as RT1138 would almost certainly also emerge with a different body. It took a long time for your average 1950s bus spotter to get his head around this system — surely RT1138 was RT1138 — and even longer for vehicle licensing authorities in other parts of Britain to understand why a former London bus no longer bore its original chassis number.

Sometimes those distant licensing people never understood it, which is why, following sale to a Lanarkshire operator, RTL12 was re-registered YVA 776 in 1960 instead of its original JXN 324.

It generally took less time to overhaul the chassis than the body, so the float system, which had existed at Chiswick before the war, was revived. Slightly more bodies were built than chassis and as soon as a chassis overhaul was completed it was fitted with the next finished body, which might be of a different type to that it carried before.

The body and chassis of Country Area STL411 being united after overhaul at Chiswick in 1947. LONDON TRANSPORT

Production line chassis overhauling at Aldenham. An RF is nearest, then an RT and an RTL. LONDON TRANSPORT

Thus some of the nominally earliest RTs, dating from 1947, might emerge with a 1954 body, or equally likely a 1950s chassis would have an early roofbox body.

This clearly confused someone at 55 Broadway who, when the disposal of the RT family began in the late 1950s so that the final 1954 vintage RTs and RTLs, then in store, could take up work, ordered that buses with the lowest numbers, i.e. from RT152 onwards, be disposed of, not realising that these might well have some of the most recent bodies.

Those who bought these bargains could hardly believe their luck, but after a while it was realised what was going on and buses with the oldest bodies were sold, a process that took decades and so thorough was an Aldenham overhaul that the nominal age of an RT was irrelevant.

Decline and closure

Both Chiswick and Aldenham went into decline with the advent of off-the-peg

buses of the post-RT and Routemaster era, overhaul of which was simply not cost effective, although many of the Merlin and Swift single-deckers, as well as the Fleetline double-deckers did not even last long enough to be overhauled. These buses were not designed for the chassis and body to be separated.

The number of employees at both establishments fell steadily away, private contract work was taken on, but this only staved off the inevitable. Aldenham works closed in 1986 and was razed to the ground in July 1996, the site now being occupied by the Centennial Business Park.

Chiswick Works suffered a similar fate, closing in 1990 following sale to private buyers. Today the site is the rather upmarket Chiswick Business Park, although the adjoining Acton Underground Railway Works still flourishes.■ **MB**

Routemasters and reshaping

The new standard double-decker became an increasingly familiar sight in the 1960s, but new ideas were being tried to keep up with the times

O n 1 January 1963, the British Transport Commission was abolished and new state-owned bodies became responsible for its component parts. The London Transport Board replaced BTC's London Transport Executive, but as in 1948 typical passengers would not have noticed any difference unless their eyes strayed down to the 1in high legal ownership details displayed on the side of each bus.

Just before this, in December 1962, Routemasters had taken over central London routes 13, 16, 36, 37 and 73 from RTs and RTLs in a process that had begun to accelerate with the completion of the trolleybus

replacement programme. That said, their predecessors still greatly outnumbered the new type.

Although the standard Routemaster seated eight more passengers than the RT or RTL and London Transport was still struggling to recruit enough staff, the crews' union refused to allow nine RMs to replace every 10 RTs or RTLs as the board had intended.

Some of the RTLs replaced the final 1940-42 RTs on driver training duties, the last of which would be sold in March 1964, while others of the Leylands were put up for sale. Postwar RTs with roof number box bodies were scheduled for early disposal, as were RTLs fitted with this type of body on overhaul, although a few survived at the end of the 1960s.

Country Area RTs were all being fitted with heaters but not roofbox ones, which were either sold or transferred to the Central Area.

The 8ft wide RTW type had been concentrated on the busiest central London routes and began to be replaced by Routemasters in 1964, but survived on route 11 until March 1966. The next month saw them disappear from the 22, another central London route, after 15 years, leaving them only at Brixton where they operated tram replacement

Routemaster RM366, new in 1960 and with the flake grey relief band applied in place of cream from 1965, in 1968. The front advertisements publicise Spencer Tracy's last film, Guess Who's Coming to Dinner, which opened on 1 February at the Leicester Square Theatre. The advertisement on the side promotes budget holidays in Germany at a time when Britons were only permitted to take £50 cash out of the country. GEOFFREY MORANT

Five of the strangest London Transport buses ever were operated by the Country Area between November 1963 and October 1965. These were the TT class Strachans-bodied Ford Thames Traders — normally a single-deck coach chassis — with 33 seats upstairs and an open area below for 23 bicycles. They provided a shuttle service for cyclists when the Dartford Tunnel opened, these hardy souls having to scale the three vertical footholds before climbing the staircase. The service was poorly used and was replaced by a Land Rover and trailer. BILL GODWIN

RLH62, one of the second batch of lowbridge Weymann-bodied AEC Regent IIIs new in 1952, spent most of its working life at Harrow Weald garage. After coming out of service in 1969, it was exported to the United States. The RLHs had the provincial version of the chassis, with taller radiator and bonnet than the RT. The advertisement for Typhoo tea uses a popular jingle on commercial television in the 1960s. OMNIBUS SOCIETY/ROY MARSHALL

routes 95 and the 109 until mid-May. More than half the 500 RTWs were sold to Ceylon.

The RT family, despite still existing in such huge numbers at the beginning of the 1960s and destined to survive into the last year of the 1970s, was becoming a leftover from a vanished era. Its design dated back to the 1939, it seated just 56 passengers and outside London the rear-engined Leyland Atlantean and Daimler Fleetline were entering service, able to carry up to 22 more passengers, who would soon be permitted to pay the driver as they got in.

London Transport's alternative was the 72-seat RML Routemaster. The first appeared in 1962 and it became the standard version from 1965 until production ended early in 1968. More comfortably appointed Routemasters were used to convert some Green Line routes to double-deck and Country Area RMLs took up work from Godstone, East Grinstead and Reigate garages from 1965.

A prototype forward-entrance version was built but never operated in London Transport service, but questions were beginning to be asked about whether the organisation or its vehicles were in tune with changing times.

Pressure for change

Back in 1955 the Chambers Committee, set up by the Ministry of Transport & Aviation, had looked at the possibility of a 'wheel plan' where suburban services would terminate at the edge of the Central Area and passengers would change to central routes. This was rejected, although another suggestion for buses with a high proportion of standing passengers on the heaviest central London traffic flows remained on the table.

With staff shortages as acute as ever, negotiations between the board and the union reached deadlock, with claims for increased pay and reduced hours being refused and in October 1963 the union urged its members to cease rest day working and overtime.

The minister of transport asked Prof Henry Phelps Brown of the London School of Economics to head a commission of inquiry. In the remarkably short time of two months it brought out an interim report on rates of pay, which found favour with the union, thus ending its restrictive actions.

The final report came out in April 1964. Its main recommendations were that experimental, larger, front-entrance double-deck one-man operated buses be introduced in central London and the Country Area, and that the standee single-deckers suggested by the Chambers Committee be introduced with flat fares and automatic fare collecting equipment.

The timing was crucial, for in 1965 London Transport would record a £1million loss. It needed to make savings and dispensing with some of its bus conductors' jobs would help deliver them.

Accordingly London Transport ordered 59 rear-engined double-deckers, the XA, XF and FRM described on the pages following this article. The eight Country

Red RF632 at Finsbury Park.
OMNIBUS SOCIETY/ROY MARSHALL

Area XFs operated without conductors from October 1966, but it was November 1969 before the Central Area followed with the first such conversion, in Croydon.

Commonwealth immigrants, some recruited directly by London Transport on campaigns in their home countries, helped reduce the impact of the continuing staff shortages, but the problem would not go away.

The days had gone when a job with London Transport conferred

RM1737, the first overall advertising in Britain as well as London, heading westbound along the Strand on route 11 at the junction with the Aldwych and Lancaster Place. OMNIBUS SOCIETY/ROY MARSHALL

considerable status on the holder and the number of scheduled journeys that had to be cancelled grew throughout the 1960s, as did tensions between board and union.

New schedules brought in at the beginning of 1966 prompted staff to ban overtime and rest day working. Around 40 services were withdrawn and over two dozen private operators were given permission to take them over, temporarily. Although London Transport took most of them back after a couple of months, the 98B in Ruislip and 235 in Richmond never did revert.

The promised standee single-deck revolution began on 18 April 1966 when six AEC Merlins took up work between Victoria and Park Lane in peak hours, to Oxford Circus at other times. The route was numbered 500, branded Red Arrow and led to other such limited stop services working between main line stations and other central points. These buses, with 25 seats and room for 48 standing passengers, were revolutionary in London but imported a decades old operating practice found on buses and trams across Europe and elsewhere.

This marked the beginning of what London Transport called its Bus Reshaping Plan, which was expected to take between 10 and 15 years to reach fruition and use buses like the Merlins. Implicit in it was the phasing out of the remaining RTs and all Routemasters. Many services would be restructured to feed into Underground stations, notably along the north-eastern route of the Victoria Line, which had been planned since 1948, under construction from 1962 and opened in September 1968.

The Bus Reshaping Programme began then and saw conversions of many routes to the new single-deckers, which displaced not only the RT family but often Routemasters too, which then replaced further RTs.

The Merlins came with great promise of a new era, but as explained on p64 they proved anything but successful and one of the less glorious episodes in the London bus story was about to unfold.

Trends and traditions

With costs rising and revenue falling, new income sources were needed and

RT745 in London Transport Board days with post-1965 flake grey band and advertising for 7/- (35p) all-day Red Rover tickets. When new in 1948, this bus had a Park Royal body with roof number box, but the Aldenham overhauling system has given it something newer. It was scrapped in 1978. OMNIBUS SOCIETY/ ROY MARSHALL

in August 1969 Routemaster RM1737 appeared repainted blue with illustrations of guardsmen and tourist attractions, all to advertise Silexine Paints.

This was the first overall advertising bus anywhere in Britain and although it went back to normal livery after a year it the started a national trend as well as a London one. But like all new

trends, it was not universally applauded and London Transport came in for an extraordinary amount of stick for daring to paint a bus in any colour other than its supposedly proper red.

Ironically, it came just as the red London bus was becoming trendy. The 1960s were when Swinging London became the cultural capital of the world, led by the Beatles from Liverpool and backed up by numerous dress shops, renamed boutiques, centred around the Kings Road and in a hitherto obscure backwater off Oxford Street called Carnaby Street.

Bus route 11 traverses the length of the Kings Road and as practically anything associated with London became a highly desirably artefact worldwide, so the London double-deck red bus became one of the most celebrated icons of the UK capital, a role it has never since relinquished.

Pop groups included it on their record covers and Twiggy, the London-born model, posed beside it. Allen Jones, one of the most eminent of the generation of Pop painters to emerge from the Royal College of Art in the early 1960s, produced paintings based on Country Area route 403.

The Country Area, however, needed more than fashionable works of art and was about to be separated from the rest of London Transport. A major reform of local government had created the Greater London Council in April 1965, sweeping away the London County Council, the county of Middlesex and absorbing some adjoining parts of Surrey, Kent and Essex. Its powers included transport and its area corresponded roughly but not entirely with that of the red bus Central Area.

So yet another change saw London Transport transferred to GLC control from January 1970, its name reverting to London Transport Executive. The Country Bus & Coach department, with its substantially loss-making bus routes and traffic-choked Green Line coaches, remained in state ownership, but as London Country Bus Services, a subsidiary of the year-old National Bus Company.

Its green buses were still largely of standard London Transport design — lots of RTs, RFs, Routemasters and quite a few GSs — but these would gradually disappear through the 1970s as it wrestled with challenges beyond the scope of this publication. ■ **MB**

The XA & XF

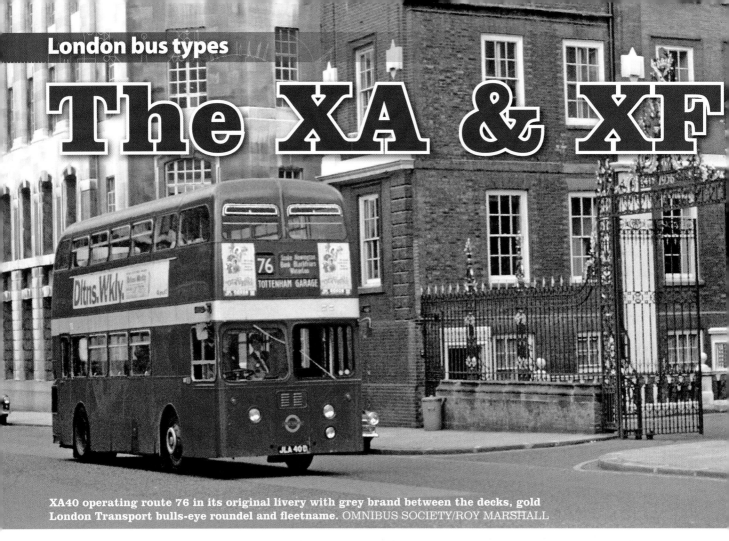

XA40 operating route 76 in its original livery with grey brand between the decks, gold London Transport bulls-eye roundel and fleetname. OMNIBUS SOCIETY/ROY MARSHALL

Just as the first production examples of London's fleet of Routemasters entered service in 1959, the shape of double-deck buses in the rest of Britain was changing thanks to a revolutionary new bus called the Leyland Atlantean.

The new orthodoxy was to have the engine mounted sideways across the back, a bit like London Transport and Leyland had pioneered 20 years earlier with the CR Cub. The main advantage when the first production Atlanteans appeared at the 1958 Commercial Motor Show — stealing all the limelight from RM8 elsewhere in Earls Court — was that by placing the driver ahead of the front wheels, he could supervise boarding and alighting and leave the conductor to collect the fares on a bus that often had as many as 78 seats.

This layout also made it possible to operate such a bus without a conductor, though it would be 1966 before one-man-operated double-deckers became legal.

Daimler, which had last supplied London Transport with wartime utility double-deckers, followed Leyland's lead with the Fleetline in 1960 and put it into production a couple of years later with the popular Gardner 6LX engine. The Fleetline had what was called a dropped rear axle, giving it a step-free floor

XA5 following its move to Croydon and repaint with white band and bulls-eye roundel only on the sides. It carries 'pay as you enter' lettering under the windscreen for one-man operation, in this case on the C2 express to the huge New Addington estate. OMNIBUS SOCIETY/ROY MARSHALL

downstairs and making it possible to build a lowheight body.

With so much invested in the Routemaster, which in all other respects was much more sophisticated than either of these back-to-front newcomers, London Transport resisted the temptation to follow the new trend. Indeed it might have been aware that the Atlantean especially could be far from trouble-

free. But with one-man operation on the horizon and pressure to adopt new ways, it bit the bullet in 1964 by ordering 58 of them as part of a wider evaluation of new experimental bus types.

There were to be 50 Atlanteans and eight Fleetlines, all given X (for experimental) fleetnumber codes. The Atlanteans were XA and were for Central Area, the Fleetlines XF and for the Country Area. Park Royal built the 72-seat bodies to one of its standard designs closely resembling double-deckers it had built for Stockton Corporation on Teesside.

Little was done to customise them for London and in the opinion of many the body was far more functional than attractive, of fairly square profile with shallow top deck windows. The opening vents on the windows on both decks were sliding, as on the Stockton buses, unlike the robust winding devices specified on the Routemaster and the RF before it.

Both buses were built to full height and to give them a level floor, the XFs had a step behind the entrance even though the chassis did not require it. This was done to improve passenger flow around the entrance and staircase, an important consideration as this part of rear-engined buses could become congested.

Mechanically, they were pretty much standard, though London Transport specified the optional higher capacity O.680 engine on the XAs rather than the more commonly purchased O.600. They had an automatic version of Leyland's Pneumo-cyclic gearbox, while the XFs had the equivalent Daimatic.

The XAs arrived in 1965/66, replacing Routemasters on route 24 (Pimlico-Hampstead Heath) from Chalk Farm garage in November 1965 and the 271 (Moorgate-Highgate Village) from Highgate in January 1966. Later in 1966, they were moved to Stamford Hill for route 67 (Northumberland Park-Wapping) and 76 (Victoria-Lower Edmonton).

There is documentary film footage of their first days in service on the 24 in Whitehall, with some confused passengers running to the back only to find an engine where they would expect there to be a door. As Gavin Booth discovered while sampling the heritage routes for this publication, things happen the other way around today, with some people seeking a non-existent door at the front of a Routemaster.

These were not the only problems to arise. In heavy traffic, the engine, flywheel and gearbox got hot, expanded and popped out bearings, causing breakdowns. Fixing that and undertaking other maintenance was time consuming and complex.

The XFs went into service at East Grinstead in September 1965, a couple of months before the XAs. They replaced RTs and also were the first to be one-man-operated, in a rather unsuccessful

trial in 1966/67 when they functioned effectively as single-deckers and the top deck was sealed off.

For comparison on two separate occasions, a different eight XAs were swapped with the green XFs at East Grinstead for operation first on the 271 and next time on the 67, with XF3 fitted experimentally with a Cummins V6 engine, which it kept until 1975.

These trials may have been sufficient to persuade London Transport that the Gardner-powered Fleetline was its better bet for future double-deck purchases. It may also have helped encourage Leyland to develop a superior version of the Atlantean, the AN68, which appeared in 1972.

By then the XA was living on borrowed time. Over the winter of 1969/70, 47 were transferred to Croydon

and Peckham to initiate one-person operation of double-deckers, while the other three went to the Country Area in the last weeks of its existence, joining the XFs in London Country ownership at its formation in January 1970. XF3 (now preserved) remained in service there until December 1981.

The reason for XA46, 47 and 48 becoming green buses was that XF6, 7 and 8 were repainted blue and silver for a new express service in Stevenage called Blue Arrow, the Atlanteans taking their place at East Grinstead.

The XAs' London career ended in 1973 when all 50 — London Transport bought back the three at London Country — were sold to China Motor Bus in Hong Kong where some are believed to have been improved by fitting Gardner engines. ■ AM

XF3 is preserved in Country Area green. The step behind the front door is visible in this picture.

The area around the foot of the staircase of X3 where London Transport modified Park Royal's body design to improve passenger flow.

The FRM

FRM1 outside its current home, the London Transport Museum's Acton Depot, in 2002 for an open day. GB

While London Transport was preparing to test its 50 XA-class Atlanteans and eight XF-class Fleetlines in service, its engineers were working with AEC and Park Royal on a rear-engined version of the Routemaster, the first — and, as it turned out, only — example being unveiled late in 1966. Even then, it seemed likely that it would remain unique, as it had been largely overtaken by events.

Carrying fleetnumber FRM1, it was clearly a member of the Routemaster family, using 60% of standard Routemaster body parts, but with its AEC AV691 engine mounted transversely at the rear. It was 9.7m (31ft 10in) long with a 72-seat one-door body. It incorporated all of the Routemaster's advanced features — aluminium integral construction, independent front suspension,

FRM1 in its final local bus service role on the town service at Potters Bar, the northernmost red bus garage. The £6 Red Bus Pass advertised on the side was valid then for one month.
GEOFFREY MORANT

hydraulic brakes and fully-automatic gearbox.

It went into service in 1967 on the busy 76 route but suffered teething troubles and a fire in the engine compartment and was duly repaired and modified, returning to the 76. In 1969 it was converted for driver-only operation and spent time working alongside XAs in Croydon, then at Potters Bar (the only garage with a route requiring a single one-person-operated double-decker) and back to central London to work on the Round London Sightseeing Tour. Even then it suffered from spells off the road, often awaiting replacement of non-standard parts.

Before it appeared, there had been rumours of FRMs for Sheffield Corporation and a couple of BET

Group companies, Northern General and Yorkshire Traction, and any surviving plans to go into production and offer the FRM on general sale were rather scuppered by the creation of British Leyland in 1968 and the many problems that massive organisation faced.

The FRM had great potential and, had circumstances permitted, it could well have gone into production and proved more successful than the first generation Atlantean and Fleetline. The doyen of bus journalists, Alan Townsin, tested FRM1 for the monthly magazine *Bus & Coach* in 1967 and wrote of 'outstanding passenger comfort' and noted that the 'ease and smooth response of driving controls reach the highest degree of refinement yet experienced on a *Bus & Coach* test'.

In some ways, the specification of the London Titan a decade later picked up on some of the main features of FRM1, including the independent front suspension and hydraulic brakes.

In a large and highly standardised fleet like London's, one-off buses tend to suffer because they are different or because they need more attention to keep them on the road. That was FRM1's fate to a certain degree, particularly after it became clear that British Leyland was not interested in building any more.

FRM1 was transferred to the London Transport Museum in 1984 and has made special appearances at various events since then, giving people the opportunity to see and sample an important 'might have been' and observe uncompleted engineering work in progress. ■ **GB**

In its original condition, as photographed on route 76 at Victoria in July 1967, FRM1 relied on mechanical ventilation and had no opening windows. This was changed shortly afterwards when a fire caused it to be taken temporarily out of service. GERALD MEAD

Final working role for the FRM was on the Round London Sightseeing Tour. Yellow doors were a feature adopted in the 1970s to direct waiting passengers to the entrance of one-person buses. OMNIBUS SOCIETY/ROY MARSHALL

The Merlin & Swift

MCW-bodied Merlin MB641, a 50-seat one-door suburban bus, is preserved in original condition.

Strachans-bodied XMS6 posed with a crush load of 'passengers' at Victoria in September 1966. LONDON TRANSPORT

There can be little doubt that the purchase of 1,453 rear-engined AEC single-deckers at the end of the 1960s was London Transport's biggest mistake with buses. It marked a sad end to an operator/manufacturer relationship that had endured two world wars and several revolutions in the development of the London bus.

The buses were purchased in great haste in response to a need to change the bus network for the advent of what then was called one-man operation — no women bus drivers in sight — and is now one-person or driver-only operation. That haste contrasts with the seven years it took to get the Routemaster from drawing board to working prototype and the further five for it to enter production.

In the meantime, AEC had changed. Its independence ended in 1962 and a merger with Leyland that was more of a takeover by its bigger competitor. One of the first fruits of that merger came in 1964 with the announcement of rear-engined single-deck city buses from both manufacturers, but sharing a chassis frame with a lower front section

to reduce the number of steps from the pavement.

They would be manufactured and branded separately, with their own engines and gearboxes, AEC's as the Swift and Leyland's as the Panther. AEC also had another product in the pipeline to be called the Merlin, but that particular heavy-duty export vehicle never materialised. But London Transport alone would apply the Merlin name to its version of the higher-powered 36ft (11m) Swift with AH690 engine.

If London later had cause to wonder if it backed the wrong Leyland group horse in this particular race, the short answer is that it did not. The Panther enjoyed no better a reputation than the Merlin/Swift. It just had the fortune not to have been bought by London Transport and to go wrong on such a visible stage.

The impetus behind developing both vehicles was that the move to 36ft single-deckers was causing a drift away from double-deckers and bus operators wanted these single-deckers to be a little more accessible — and therefore quicker away from bus stops — than

was possible when the engine was in the middle and the floor had to be built above it for the entire length of the bus. Widespread staff shortages also were encouraging a move to one-man operation and before 1966 that only was possible with single-deckers.

With both models, chassis units from existing mid underfloor-engined single-deckers were transplanted into the new lower frame, probably without a huge amount of punishing testing.

Needed in a hurry

In London, the Phelps-Brown recommendations had led to agreement for an extension of one-man operation

and the trial introduction of 'standee' single-deckers — a euphemism for a design in which substantial numbers of passengers would stand at busy times.

It needed these buses in a hurry and if AEC and Leyland had developed them with undue impatience, London Transport compounded it by ordering them virtually untested.

The initial order had the proportions of a toe in the water: 15 Merlins of which six (class XMS — Experimental Merlin Standee) with 25 seats at the back and space for 48 standees for the first Red Arrow route in central London; nine 46-seaters (XMB — B for Bus) for the Country Area. All would have two-door bodies by Strachans (pronounced 'Strawns') in Hampshire with a front end similar to the RF.

The XMS had turnstiles operated by sixpenny (2.5p) coins and issued no tickets. They went into service on 18 April 1966 on Red Arrow route 500. The XMBs went nowhere, thanks to a union embargo on their operation and eight were converted to XMS standard in 1967.

Thus far, this was all still a promising experiment. In September 1966, London Transport published its Bus Reshaping Plan that ushered in a move towards large-scale one-man operation, self-service fare collection and satellite

Inside an XMS, the turnstiles leading to the standing area and then the 25 seats in the raised section at the back. LONDON TRANSPORT

MBA588 was the sole example painted in this experimental livery in 1972. OMNIBUS SOCIETY/ROY MARSHALL

routes radiating from suburban and local district centres. Having the plan, it was keen to implement it and placed an order for another 150 Merlins.

These were to come in four layouts: Red Arrow (MBA), two-door Country bus (MB), one-door Central Area suburban bus (also MB) and two-door suburban Central Area flat fare bus (MBS).

The order was probably beyond the resources of a small bodybuilder like Strachans, so it went instead to Metro-Cammell Weymann, its first large London contract since the RF and RT. Although largely similar in appearance to the Strachans body, its design had more modern looking curved windscreens and some structural changes. They began arriving in 1967 but it was 1968 before most went into service.

A further 450 of all four variants were ordered before many of the first 150 saw much if any use and all 600 were delivered by October 1969.

Country Area MB90 is preserved with the yellow waistband used to identify one-man buses. AM

Such was the volume of Merlins being built that MCW had to subcontract some orders from other operators and lose others to competitors.

Problems surface

Mechanical and structural problems had become apparent within a short time of their entry intro service. Their engines seem to have been reasonably robust but other areas were less so and the bodies — in common with many contemporary two-door rear-engined single-deckers — were unable to withstand the flexing of the long chassis frame.

Park Royal-bodied Swift SMS445 at Bushey in June 1976. It was sold to Citybus in Belfast two years later and scrapped in 1981. TONY WILSON

MCW-bodied Swift SMS816, new at the end of 1971, operating at Loughton in July 1976. It went into store at the end of 1978 and was sold for scrap. TONY WILSON

Added to this, their length proved too great for parts of some routes, causing delays and accident damage.

So when it ordered another 148 single-deckers, it was decreed that these and future orders would be for the shorter 33ft 5in (11m) version, which London Transport called Swifts. There would be three versions, single-door Central Area (SM), two-door Country (also SM) and Central Area suburban standee (SMS).

Essentially these were scaled down versions of the Merlin with a similar-looking body with altered side window mountings and fewer seats. They would have AEC's smaller AH505 engine. Bodies for the initial order would come from Marshall and Park Royal. The first, with Marshall body, arrived in November 1969.

A further 390 were ordered in 1969 including 90 with MCW bodies for the Country Area and in 1970 a final 300 were ordered for the Country-free London Transport, all with MCW bodies,

with the final examples arriving in February 1972. All 138 ordered for the Country Area were delivered after it became London Country Bus Services, joining 109 Merlins already there.

Although many of the faults in the Merlins were cured in the Swifts, they brought their own mechanical and structural challenges and both types also fell foul of nationwide shortages of spare parts.

End of the line

What killed the Merlin fleet finally was its incompatibility with the Aldenham overhauling system. Not having been built with Aldenham in mind, they were going to be too expensive to rebuild there and the decision instead was taken to take all of them out of service as they fell due for major attention. Space was rented at Radlett airfield to accommodate them pending sale.

The only exceptions were the Red Arrow MBAs, which survived on

those routes until new replacements arrived in May 1981. Twelve years for a London bus may have compared badly with the older types, but by comparison with the other Merlins it was a long time.

Many went for scrap after service in London, though some did find new working homes, most notably in Northern Ireland where the state-owned Ulsterbus and Citybus companies needed replacements for vehicles being destroyed in the depths of the Troubles and which might themselves be destroyed, which several were.

The Swifts started to be sold in October 1976, with many of these also going to Northern Ireland while others were destined to have long (and massively rebuilt) lives in Malta. The last came out of suburban service at Edgware in January 1981, the last of all from Red Arrow work in July the same year. ■ **AM**

Victoria
Aldwych **11**
Fulham Broadway

Route 11

King's Road, Chelsea.

The 11 is one of the oldest bus routes in London, and arguably one of the most famous. Some tourist publications rightly commend it as a cheap way to see some of the most popular sights.

It dates back to 1906, which makes it even older than the 1 (by a couple of years). What's more, it hasn't changed much over the years, except in detail. At its western extremity it once ran up to Shepherd's Bush, whereas now it terminates at Fulham Broadway, about 2 miles to the south; but that's about it.

It's essentially an east-west route now. We follow it eastwards, and subjectively it feels as if it's in central London for almost the whole of the ride — passing many of picture postcard landmarks on its 7 mile journey.

The operator is Go-Ahead London General, which from 21 September 2013 will use three-door New Bus for London double-deckers. When we rode it, the buses were nicely turned-out Volvo B7TLs with Wright Eclipse Gemini bodies in the group's full London livery (grey skirt panels,

yellow lining). Many are at least 10 years old, but they don't show their age — except in hot weather, when the engine cooling fan kicks in, and is apt to increase the normally subdued engine note to an undignified roar.

The vast majority of these buses retain multi-destination indicators, though they list only two intermediate stops these days — Aldwych and Victoria — not the panoply of iconic locations shown 10 years ago when Routemasters still held sway on the route: Chelsea, Charing Cross, Fleet Street, Bank.

Diving briefly south from Fulham Broadway, the 11 quickly turns left on to New King's Road, which merges into King's Road proper after negotiating an extended chicane called World's End (after a pub of the same name). This area was the height of chic in the 1960s, though the trendy area has retreated somewhat to the true King's Road today.

Once in the heart of Chelsea we pass the gleaming art deco Bluebird restaurant (once a garage), then Chelsea Town Hall and countless boutiques. Finally the buildings grow in stature, culminating in the striking

1930s Peter Jones department store on the corner of Sloane Square.

From here we weave our way through to Buckingham Palace Road, where we pass between two imposing 1930s office blocks — the former BOAC Air Terminal to our right, Victoria Coach Station to our left. Then round the one-way system at Victoria station, skirting round the bus

Left: One of the oldest Wright-bodied Volvo B7TLs in the Go-Ahead London General fleet operating a westbound 11 in the Strand, with the church of St Mary Le Strand behind.

The Peter Jones store at Sloane Square.

station itself, and off along Victoria Street to Parliament Square.

Westminster Cathedral slides by on the right, with its patterned brickwork more visible following adjacent demolition in recent decades; then Westminster Abbey and the Houses of Parliament.

Up Whitehall now, past Edward Lutyens's elegantly spare Cenotaph (commemorating the fallen in World War 1); past patient tourists seeking a glimpse of Downing Street on the left; and into Trafalgar Square, though we merely brush a corner of it, since traffic remodelling means it's no longer a roundabout.

Next we're heading east again along the Strand, past theatres to either side. At the Aldwych one-way system we pass not one but two Restoration churches, both captive in an island position — Christopher Wren's St Clement Danes and James Gibbs's slightly later St Mary Le Strand. If you keep an eye out on the return journey you can also spot the disused Aldwych tube station entrance, which lies at the end of a short spur off the Piccadilly Line, running south from Holborn. On the red terracotta fascia it bears the original name of Stand station.

From here we pass the extraordinary 1870s Law Courts, looking rather inappropriately like a fairy palace, and we enter Fleet Street. This has changed little in recent decades, though the newspapers that were once based here disappeared 20 years ago or more, and now mostly live in Docklands. But their imposing offices remain — especially the former

Telegraph building of 1928, finished in classical style in Portland stone, and the former *Express* building, with its curving art deco chromium and black glass, completed just three years later.

St Paul's comes next, at the top of a modest rise called Ludgate Hill. Tourists mill around, or simply laze in the sun. Then we progress into the City, approaching the Bank of England via Cannon Street and Queen Victoria Street. Tourists thin out, the streets narrow down and buildings grow taller. Apart from Docklands, this is one of the few places where central London has true skyscrapers.

The architecture here is a mix of traditional and unashamedly modern, but somehow it all seems to work together. Grand vistas are few, but you get teasing glimpses of notable buildings like Norman Foster's Gherkin (actually 30 St Mary Axe). And finally we arrive at the 11's eastern terminus, Liverpool Street station — elegantly modernised in recent years to make the best of its unadorned Victorian façade. ■ **PR**

Big Ben and Parliament Square.

An eastbound number 11 at St Paul's.

Passing Victoria Coach Station, opened in 1932 and owned and operated by Transport for London since 1988.

It was just our cup of tea

ANDREW BRADDOCK recalls the wide range of products and extra curricular activities once available to all London Transport employees

Someone once described life at London Transport as being from cradle to the grave and my experience of working within the organisation twice (1966-68 and 1991-2000 extending into the Transport for London era until 2003) suggests that was not far wrong.

I managed to find my original appointment letter from the hallowed 55 Broadway, London SW1, and you will see that London Transport took me on in 1966 at a princely salary of £485 per annum. More importantly, the letter refers to my being required to join the contributory superannuation fund and that is something I have cause to be grateful for as a Transport for London pensioner nowadays, from what may turn out to be the UK's only generation of beneficiaries of a final salary pension scheme.

Notice also that the letter mentions my eligibility for a free travel pass on all London Transport's rail and bus services (including country services and Green Line coaches) and for 'privilege' tickets on British Railways.

The first of these had considerable value, of course (not least to those of us who enjoyed travelling around the vast network our passes covered), but the second was a real bonus as it enabled quarter-rate, and sometimes free, travel on most continental European railways. I can recall several jaunts to the Low Countries, France, Germany and Italy — and even a long weekend marathon to Athens — on the back of these generous concessions.

Holders of so-called 'Priv' tickets could also benefit from membership of Repta — the Railway Employees' Privilege Trading Association — which sourced all manner of deals from insurance to bedroom furniture, all set out in a handy catalogue.

Furthermore, there was a plethora of offers made through London Transport's canteens to its staff which I certainly took advantage of — notably the incredibly cheap gallon cans of Teepol which was basically Fairy washing-up liquid by another name.

Almost every morning between March 1966 and November 1968 (when I left London Transport and moved to Bath, to join the then Bristol Omnibus Company) my conscience and I would debate whether to have a second cup of tea or head for the Tube (and work).

As the Bakerloo (now Jubilee) Line offered a train every 3min or so to get me to Baker Street (for the Chiltern Court offices of the Estate & Rating Surveyor — intriguingly mis-spelt as Chilton Court in the appointment letter) it was not hard for me to win the argument and indulge in another delicious Griffin tea. This was the brand name for London

London Transport's own brand cup that cheered.
LONDON TRANSPORT MUSEUM

Transport's home-produced range used in the canteens and sold to staff.

I used to imagine a smartly dressed official in the early days of the London Passenger Transport Board going out to colonial Ceylon and India to source directly the best in leaf tea and purchase vast quantities for shipment straight to the Food Production Centre at Croydon.

This vital component in London Transport's very own food chain produced meat pies and apple tarts along with a cornucopia of other edible delights, and I went there once on a staff visit.

Now these were another benefit of being part of the rather paternalistic, but vast, organisation that was the London Transport of the 1950s to the 1970s, and jolly good they were too. The idea was to take mixed groups drawn from a variety of departments to both internal and outside venues, such as Aldenham Works and the Rank Xerox photocopier factory in the Forest of Dean — both of which I participated in during my 1966-68 sojourn.

Mention should also be made of the 'out of work' activities available to staff — colleagues tried in vain to sign me up for membership of the LT Players amateur dramatic society and the LT Rugby Club, to name but two of the array of similar opportunities to extend one's interests.

Just the ticket?

Self-sufficiency was the order of the day and it was rumoured that the

L O N D O N   T R A N S P O R T
55 BROADWAY, WESTMINSTER, LONDON, S.W.1

ABBey 5600   Travel enquiries: ABBey 1234   Telegrams: Passengers Sowest

Extension 321
Our reference T.11/RM
Your reference ARM.E.

24th January, 1966

Dear Mr. Braddock,

With reference to your application for employment and to your subsequent interview here, I am pleased to offer you a class B appointment in the office of the Estate and Rating Surveyor. Chilton Court at a commencing salary of £485 per annum. This offer is subject to the general regulations applicable to the clerical staff of the Board, including the receipt of satisfactory references and a medical examination.

You would be eligible for a pass which would enable you to travel free on London Transport's railways, central buses and country buses. In addition after one month's service, you would become eligible for privilege tickets entitling you to reduced rate travel on British Railways.

You would be on probation in the first instance and after not more than twelve months, provided that you had proved satisfactory, you would be established and required to join a contributory Superannuation Fund.

Will you please confirm your acceptance of this offer and if so, when you can attend for a medical examination. This can be arranged any morning between 8.30 and 11.00 a.m. (except Saturday) upon telephoning my office (Extension 321).

Yours faithfully,

J A Neale

170

J.A. Neale
STAFF AND TRAINING OFFICER

Mr. A. J. Braddock,
68, Blenheim Gardens,
Willesden Green,
London, N. W. 2.

Andrew Braddock's appointment letter welcoming him to the great organisation.

ticket machine works at Effra Road, Brixton, were turned over every last Friday of the month to the production of toilet rolls.

The cutting machines which were normally loaded with huge bales of paper to churn out ticket rolls for Gibson machines were apparently set to wider margins to slice up a different kind of paper and stamp each sheet with 'London Transport' at the top and 'Now wash your hands' at the bottom.

This urban legend was extended by one wag to suggest that 'In the interests of economy, please use both sides' might have been added to

London Transport toilet rolls during the World War 2. Around 10 years later I discovered at London Country Bus Services (separated from London Transport in 1970) that most of the company's garages had sufficient stocks of its former owner's toilet paper to last into the 1980s.

I think I was lucky to be a very small part of the huge LT 'family' during what was its heyday — an organisation unique in the UK — and I am delighted now to be a committee member of The 55 Society, which brings together more than 400 of its former managers at well-attended lunches throughout the year. ∎

The wheels work loose

Council control projected London Transport more firmly in the political arena than at any time before or since — a period when the organisation also celebrated its own golden jubilee

The end of the most standardised London bus fleet ever. On 7 April 1979, RT624 — the last of a family of nearly 7,000 double-deckers built mainly between 1947 and 1954 — returns to Barking garage, surrounded by enthusiasts and local wellwishers. There had been an RT624 since August 1948, though the Aldenham overhaul system meant there probably was little of the original on this one nearly 31 years later. It had even changed colour, RT624 having been a green Country Area bus until emerging in red in April 1965.
OMNIBUS SOCIETY/ROY MARSHALL

Buoyed along by such human achievements as America's landing of the first men on the Moon in 1969 and the prospect of a modern new decimal currency in 1971, Britain entered the 1970s with a sense of optimism that the progress of the 1950s and 1960s would not only be sustained but might accelerate.

Instead, the new decade was clouded by industrial discord, economic decline and double-digit inflation. The wheels seemed to be coming off the postwar boom and if they were not coming off the slightly slimmed-down Country Area-free London

Transport, they certainly were looking shaky.

The new Merlin single-deckers were proving structurally troublesome, as well as too long for some routes. The shorter AEC Swifts bought to continue the move to one-person operation would bring their own forms of grief, convincing some in the organisation that there was no substitute for a bespoke London bus designed for the rigours and operating practices of the capital.

Such vehicles had ceased to be built with the end of Routemaster production. Now London Transport was buying what it termed 'off-the-peg' buses: manufacturers' standard vehicles available to everyone, but tailored to London needs especially in the design and internal layout of the bodywork and in the way that the drivers' cabs were arranged. In that sense, they were no more off-the-peg than had been the prewar STL, except that their chassis lacked the benefit of this major operator's input.

The first of the Swifts entered service in January 1970. Their double-deck equivalent, the DMS-class Daimler Fleetline, began arriving towards the end of the year and went into service early in 1971.

As explained in the articles starting on pages 64 and 78, the London experience with these rear-engined buses was spectacularly bad, prompting the early disposal of almost all of them. Its single-deck experience was not unique: other operators had serious problems with many of theirs, though they had far fewer of them than London Transport.

There also was a widespread national shortage of spare parts, with British Leyland, which had a near monopoly of the market for heavy-duty buses, unable to meet demand. This also interrupted the supply of new vehicles.

The other side of that same coin was that the buses the new ones were supposed to replace — RTs, RFs and Routemasters — all were retained much longer than planned and beyond their design lives. In the case of the RTs and RFs, the cost of keeping such relative veterans on the road was higher than could possibly be justified, though allowance must be made for the shortcomings of the troublesome new vehicles.

The last RTs and RFs finally came off in spring 1979, around the same time as London Transport was buying back Routemasters lost to London Country at the start of the decade.

Coupled with the problems with newer buses, London Transport also began questioning its own wisdom in converting routes to one-person operation. Despite its efforts to automate fare collection with self-service ticket machines and turnstile barriers, the removal of conductors was slowing services down. Many, perhaps most, passengers preferred to pay the driver than use the complicated and unreliable slot machines.

And having been a late convert to double-deckers with doors that opened only at bus stops, it could — and did — frequently quote statistics arguing that the service

was far faster with an open-platform Routemaster.

It seemed to blow hot and cold over the wisdom of employing or not employing conductors and by 1974 — having about 40% of the fleet made up of one-person buses — was specifying Fleetlines for use with conductors. This despite the fact that the buses qualified for a 50% capital grant from central government made available originally to accelerate the phasing out of conductors and buses with a Routemaster layout that demanded a conductor.

A couple of years later, it bowed to public and political pressure and stopped accepting overall advertising on its buses. Since the Silexene Routemaster of 1969/70, 27 Routemasters and a Merlin had carried various schemes advertising all manner of products including wine, beer, sweets, football pools and toothbrushes.

More political control

The end of overall advertising — it returned spasmodically in later years — was the thin end of an exceptionally thick wedge of political control that was a hallmark of the years when London Transport reported to and relied upon financial support from the Greater London Council.

Transport was one of the GLC's main areas of responsibility and arguably the one most Londoners recognised as a service they used. Over the 22 years that it existed, there were six elections to the council and every one of them was won

Among the secondhand Routemasters that London Transport bought in the 1970s were the 65 forward-entrance vehicles operated on behalf of British Airways (originally British European Airways) between the West London Air Terminal and Heathrow Airport. They formed an RMA class. A few ran briefly in public service but they were used mainly as driver trainers or staff buses. The trainers, like RMA42, retained seats upstairs but had the staircases removed so an instructor's seat could go behind the driver's cab. An extra window was fitted for the instructor, replacing a plain metal panel. OMNIBUS SOCIETY/ROY MARSHALL

Strachans-bodied Ford Transit FS5 in Brixton on one of the four minibus routes introduced in 1972. OMNIBUS SOCIETY/ROY MARSHALL

by the party in opposition to the national government: Labour in 1964, 1973 and 1981, Conservative in 1967, 1970 and 1977.

One effect of this was for the council to intervene in such matters as fares levels, putting increasing strain on the personal relationship between London Transport's top management and the council's leaders. In 1972, the Conservatives limited a proposed increase. The following year, Labour imposed a fares freeze but in 1975 increased them by 60% to make good losses made worse by 25% inflation that year.

While London began tackling some of the traffic congestion problems by starting to install bus lanes, and restricted the western part of Oxford Street to buses and taxis, the GLC sometimes wavered in its commitment to them, especially when the motorists' vote looked risky.

A mooted Speedbus network of at least 10 limited stop routes along substantial sections of near-continuous bus lanes and priorities, first proposed in 1973 in hopes of implementation the next year, fell foul of objections.

On the other hand, the GLC provided the impetus for the introduction in 1972 of four new local routes — in Enfield, Hampstead, Bromley and Dulwich — using 20 Ford Transit 16-seat minibuses to penetrate the narrow streets of residential areas and extend the coverage of the bus network. These routes all developed into permanent fixtures, though bigger buses took the place of the Transits, which lacked the durability of a 'proper' London bus. They were the first London buses in the best part of 15 years to have manual gearboxes.

Some London Transport routes ran beyond the GLC area into surrounding counties and as costs rose and passenger numbers reduced, it sought financial support from those councils to keep some of them running. They did not always agree and in some cases, notably in Surrey, London Country — the old Country Area — provided reduced replacements at substantially lower cost, increasing the penetration of green buses in red bus territory.

There also were a few places served by private operators, among them the outer suburbs connecting Orpington and Croydon where Orpington & District ran until 1981, then Tillingbourne (Metropolitan) until it reformed as Metrobus in 1983.

Twenty-year-old Routemaster RM59 westbound on Brompton Road past Harrods in 1979 during the six months of the Shop Linker service. Besides the bus and ubiquitous FX4 black taxis, most cars on the road were still British. A Hillman Super Minx not much newer than RM59 heads towards town with an impressive load of luggage on its roof rack. Opposite, a bronze Rolls-Royce is parked behind an Austin Allegro estate. RM59, restored to standard red livery, survived another 10 years before being scrapped. AM

A lowbridge Weymann-bodied Leyland Atlantean of Orpington & District, new to Maidstone & District in 1959, loading in Croydon around 20 years later on the Orpington service that complemented London Transport coverage in the area. In 2013, services on this corridor are part of the Transport for London network. AM

Better buses, sponsored buses

The first hint that better buses might be coming was in May 1976, when a prototype Leyland Titan began operational trials on crew-operated route 24. This bus was red, but never a London Transport vehicle, but emblazoned with the manufacturer's own branding.

Although not designed exclusively for London, the Titan benefited from a great deal of London Transport engineering input, to the extent that it appeared over-specified for most other operators at the time. Five of the comparable Metrobus

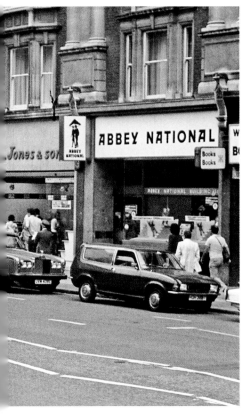

Routemaster RM595 with Heinz sponsorship for the 1981 royal wedding. OMNIBUS SOCIETY/ ROY MARSHALL

from Metro-Cammell Weymann followed a couple of years later and both types became the standard London double-decker until 1984.

Overall advertising buses may have become a no-no, but commercially sponsored commemorative liveries were something else. For the Queen's silver jubilee, 25 Routemasters were painted silver, given temporary fleetnumbers SRM1-25 and subtle advertising for products like alcohol, tobacco, batteries, computers, retailers, watches and carpets.

A repeat exercise two years later, when London Transport celebrated 150 years since George Shillibeer's horsebus began the first recognisable bus service in the capital, involved 13 buses — 12 Routemasters and a Fleetline — in a representation of Shillibeer's ornate green and cream livery.

The Fleetline — DM2646, the last one

built for London — was sponsored by Leyland and publicised the Titan. The manufacturer did not want to endorse its new London bus on one of the oldest ones and really wanted a Shillibeer Titan, only London Transport was playing safe then by operating all its new double-deckers in the outer suburbs and not in the centre where the sponsored buses needed to be.

There were eight sponsors for the Routemasters, North Thames Gas paying for five of them. This may have been a sign of diminishing returns from sponsored liveries or simply that the national economy was still in recession. When a similar opportunity arose for the wedding of Prince Charles and Lady Diana Spencer in 1981, just eight Routemasters attracted sponsorship for their red livery with silver painted ribbons.

There had also been 16 Routemasters operated from April until September 1979 on Shop Linker, a clockwise and anticlockwise circular service via Marble Arch, Oxford Circus, Piccadilly Circus, South Kensington, Notting Hill Gate and Lancaster Gate. Despite the buses being painted eye-catching red and yellow, the service did not catch on.

In 1983, 10 buses carried special liveries to commemorate 50 years of London Transport. Routemaster RM1983 and Titan T747 (renumbered for the duration as T1983, there not being that number of Titans in the fleet) were gold for this golden jubilee. Four Routemasters (one of them RM1933) and Fleetline DS1933 were given 1933-style red and white, a Titan and Metrobus the same colours with General names. And another Fleetline carried Croydon Corporation brown and cream tram colours.

The rollercoaster ride

Such celebrations were but a sideshow to the political rollercoaster ride with the GLC that London Transport experienced from 1981 and that led to its return to state ownership.

The Labour administration elected that year was of a more radical political stripe than those that held office in the 1960s and 1970s, with newly appointed leader Ken Livingstone very quickly pitching the council into a battle of ideas with the equally radical Conservative government of Margaret Thatcher. Together with his transport committee chair, former London busman Dave Wetzel, he put public transport at the sharp end of the battle.

Labour was elected on a pledge to cut fares and in October 1981 a 32% reduction

to 1969 levels was accompanied by a move to zonal flat fares; in the outer suburban zone introduced when the Conservatives ran the GLC, the cut was from 25p to 20p. There also was a 10p 'short hop' for short distance travel.

There was to be no extension of one-person operation and the new administration talked of commissioning a new Routemaster built in London.

To fund the fares cut, the GLC levied a precept on ratepayers. The 32 London boroughs collected rates, including the proportion payable to the GLC, and Conservative-controlled Bromley challenged the precept in the courts, arguing among other things that as British Rail had declined to be part of the fares cut and the borough had no Underground lines, its property-owning residents were paying to subsidise a service they did not receive.

The case went to the House of Lords — then the highest court in the land — where the GLC lost in December 1981. For a time there were doubts whether any public transport subsidies were legal. Fares almost doubled in March 1982, but with the multi-journey Travelcard introduced to take some of the sting out of it, and some services were reduced, triggering the volume withdrawal of Routemasters for the first time.

The GLC and London Transport subsequently went to court to establish the legality of a 25% fares reduction, which took effect from May 1983.

By then, the government was moving towards ultimate abolition of the GLC and in a first move took away its responsibilities for transport. A House of Commons select committee had proposed something akin to the original London Passenger Transport Board, a metropolitan transport authority for much of the London commuter area with powers to levy charges on ratepayers. It suggested it be called London Regional Transport.

The body set up to take London Transport back into state ownership on 29 June 1984 was indeed called London Regional Transport, but it lacked the tax-raising powers that the MPs had wanted and its remit continued to end somewhere around the M25 orbital motorway.

Towards the end of GLC control, the council had appointed its own additional nominees to the London Transport board to help implement its policies. Among its legacies was a watertight advertising contract opposing the council's abolition, which finally happened in 1986. ■ **AM**

Route 24

Pimlico 24

oute 24 is unusual in
having hardly changed
in length or alignment
in more than 100 years.
In many ways it's a north-south
equivalent to the east-west 11. It's
about the same length (7miles) and
like the 11 it doesn't venture all that
far from central London in either
direction. What it does is scythe
through some of the most famous parts
of the capital's West End.

By the time you read this, the buses
on this route will have changed. As we
go to print, they are Volvos with Wright
Eclipse Gemini 2 bodywork, less than a
year old; but this route was earmarked
as the first to be run entirely by the
new LT-class —otherwise known as the
New Bus for London or 'Borismaster'
(after London Mayor Boris Johnson,
who championed it). These were due on

22 June 2013, so our pictures show a
bit of short-lived history.

The operator is Metroline, which for
more than 12 years has been part of
Singapore-based ComforDelGro, one of
the world's biggest bus companies. The
fleet we saw and rode on was made up of
mostly conventional B9TLs, along with a
handful of hybrid-drive Volvo B5LHs. The
two types look similar, and we couldn't
detect much difference between them in
travelling experience either, although the
hybrids' engines cut out at some stops
and pull away quietly in electric before the
diesel bursts back into life.

Is the ride smoother than on older
B7TLs? At times we thought so, but that
could just have been down to better roads
or smoother driving.

At its southern end, the 24 starts from
the Grosvenor Road, which forms part
of the Thames embankment just east of

Chelsea. Then it turns north into Pimlico,
a land of white porticoed terraces. These
look like their more upmarket equivalents
in Belgravia, a little to the north, but
many have been converted into small
hotels, flats or bedsits.

From here the 24 weaves its way north
to Victoria, then round the complicated
one-way system there, eastwards along
Victoria Street to Parliament Square, and
north again up Whitehall to Trafalgar
Square. We describe these sections of the
journey in the articles on routes 3 and 11.

Passing the imposing pillared façade of
St Martins-in-the-Fields, we head directly
north up Charing Cross Road — past
the Garrick Theatre and Capital Radio
and on to Hippodrome Corner, providing
glimpses of Leicester Square to the left
and Covent Garden to the right.

Then onward across Cambridge Circus,
where Charing Cross Road is crossed

**One of Metroline's Volvo B9TLs
crossing the Regent's Canal
in Camden with a northbound
24, where it feels as though
everyone is on holiday.**

Hampstead Heath 24

The elegant hotels of Pimlico.

Camden Market, a great place to meet.

diagonally by Shaftesbury Avenue; past music shops and bookshops; and into Tottenham Court Road, host to the oversized Dominion Theatre, Goodge Street station, Heals' furniture store and numerous electric discount shops.

Then we cross the Euston Road dual carriageway, overlooked by Euston Tower, one of the West End's few skyscraper blocks (and former home to Capital Radio), and by the gleaming new University College Hospital. This can be a slow junction at the best of times, made slower today by road works.

Heading on northwards, we pass the massive and striking Greater London House, which was built in 1928 in exuberant art deco style as a tobacco factory (the façade still bears the Carreras name), and was the first building in the country using pre-stressed concrete. It's now offices.

Mornington Crescent station, opened in 1907. Like many at the time, it was built as plinth in hopes that developers would build property above.

Then we reach Mornington Crescent, whose tube station is famed by the spoof game on the Radio 4 programme *I'm Sorry, I Haven't a Clue*. It's one of 40 with a surface building designed by Leslie Green in the early 1900s and faced in glazed ox-blood terracotta tiles, but one of just three with 'listed' status. There are two parallel branches of the Northern Line here, but to travellers' eternal bafflement, the station serves only one of them.

A little farther north we climb Camden High Street into Camden Town, which seems for all the world like a self-contained town centre: a real surprise, so close to central London. Then beyond Camden Town tube station the road takes on the quality of a street market; small boutiques vie with each other for attention and compete with the stalls in Camden Market itself. There's a festive, bohemian air about the place; it feels as though everyone is on holiday.

Over a bridge crossing elegant Camden Lock, under a heavy iron railway bridge, and we're out into Chalk Farm, a pleasant suburbia of town houses and Victorian flats. Finally the 24 wends its way up past the Royal Free Hospital and on to the terminus, just short of Hampstead Heath, where buses turn round at a leafy little square called South End Green.

A real curiosity here is a tramwaymen's shelter — a green wooden shed owned by Transport for London (pictured below), serving as a café for bus drivers during their layover. Remarkably, it's a Grade 2 listed building, erected in the 1890s to the same pattern as the dozen or so cabmen's shelters still scattered around central London. And it's still in use. ■ **PR**

80 years of capital service

77

The Fleetline & Metropolitan

For its return to buying double-deckers from 1970, London Transport purchased 2,646 rear-engined Daimler and Leyland Fleetlines. Daimler had launched the Fleetline in 1960 and it became a Leyland product around 1974, six years after Daimler became part of newly created British Leyland.

Experience with the XA and XF had persuaded London Transport that the Fleetline was the better of the two, so it was not a major surprise when it ordered a cautious 17 for 1969 delivery, although delivery delays meant that they only appeared in 1970, by which time another 350 had been ordered.

They had rather square-rigged versions of what had become a standard double-deck body style used by several of the principal bodybuilders, increasingly found on new buses throughout the UK including customised versions for the Passenger Transport Executives in Greater Manchester, West Midlands and West Yorkshire.

In an allover red livery the new London Fleetlines perhaps looked less attractive than their provincial cousins but later white bands or upper deck window surrounds helped their appearance. The engine compartment at the back was shrouded to give the rear profile a squarer look.

The new buses, type DMS, had two doors — a front door leading to automatic fare collection equipment and a centre exit door. In other words, this was a shorter but twin-floor version of the Swift and Merlin single-deckers. They had just 68 seats, with only 24 seats on the lower deck and space for 24 standing passengers.

There was an attempt to give them a catchy name in the mould of the

MCW-bodied DMS2205 survived in service longer than any of the Fleetlines with standard chassis, as it was fitted experimentally with a Maxwell gearbox in 1983. This picture was taken at Chipstead Valley three years later. AM

Routemaster: the Londoner. Ralph Bennett, London Transport's managing director (buses), had previously been general manager of Manchester Corporation's buses and its new double-deckers a couple of years earlier were called Mancunian. The Londoner name did not catch on.

As the first examples went into service early in January 1971, London Transport was ordering a further 1,600 Fleetlines, bringing the total orders at that time to 1,967 buses. Unfortunately, the early 1970s was not a good time for bus production as chassis builders, engine manufacturers and bodybuilders

Rear view of Park Royal-bodied DM2646, the last Fleetline delivered to London Transport, restored by Ensignbus to the livery it wore in 1979 to celebrate the 150th anniversary of George Shillibeer's first bus service. This shows the cooling 'chimneys' on the B20 Fleetlines. AM

got seriously out of synch with each other and long delivery delays resulted.

The first DMSs had Gardner's popular and powerful 6LXB engine, though the order for 1,600 was split between the 6LXB and Leyland's 680 engine and the bodywork order between Park Royal and Metro-Cammell Weymann, both builders with a long tradition of supplying London's needs.

Central London routes were still dominated by crew-operated Routemasters and in 1973 London Transport decided that it would not convert any more Central London routes to driver-only operation and specified a proportion of its 1974 delivery as DM types, designed for crew operation and

The Scania Metropolitan

Metropolitan MD16 at Crystal Palace in August 1982. AM

If many of the Fleetlines had remarkably short lives in London — remember that the previous standard double-deck types often clocked up 25-30 years in regular use — then the Scania/MCW Metropolitans fared worse and barely managed eight.

MCW had tied up a deal with Swedish manufacturer to build its single-deck city bus in Birmingham from 1969, calling it the Metro-Scania, and went on to develop the Metropolitan double-deck equivalent in 1973. Both had an 11.1litre engine, air suspension and a torque converter automatic transmission. They were quiet, smooth riding if a little bouncy and had the rapid acceleration of a trolleybus.

London Transport had bought six Metro-Scanias (MS1-6) in 1973 to test alongside the new Leyland National, but took them out of service in 1976 and sold them a couple of years later.

MCW-bodied D1828 at Kings Cross with a logo for Abbey District next to the door. London Buses devolved some day-to-day responsibilities districts from December 1979. The D class were previously crew-operated DM buses adapted for driver-only operation.
OMNIBUS SOCIETY/ROY MARSHALL

Leyland in Lancashire, which caused some hiccups in production and some switching of engine types and bodybuilders to ensure a continuous supply of new buses. The volume of the London Fleetline orders kept Daimler/Leyland, MCW and Park Royal busy in the early 1970s, which caused problems for other operators looking for new buses and caused some to switch suppliers.

London's last Fleetline orders were placed for 1974/75 delivery and totalled 679 buses, of which 279 would be standard types with the other 400 to a new B20 specification, with a turbocharged Leyland 690 engine. This had been developed to reduce engine noise and externally the buses had 'chimneys' replacing the engine shrouds at the rear. At the same time it also ordered 164 Scania/MCW Metropolitan double-deckers.

The last standard Fleetlines were delivered in mid-1977 and the last of the quiet B20s just a year later, bringing the type total to 2,646, just short of the 2,760 iconic Routemasters.

Even before these final Fleetline deliveries were made London Transport was admitting that the type was 'not a complete success' and saying that no more would be ordered.

Some of the rot had set in as early as 1976, when the earliest examples were due their first major overhaul. The intention was for Aldenham Works to separate the body and chassis just like on an RT, but it seems that nobody had asked Park Royal to make this possible and those bodies would distort if removed. The MCW bodies could be separated but it was decided to overhaul all of them as complete vehicles.

Besides, gearbox and brake failures were occurring much earlier than on other double-deckers and other problems were manifesting themselves, pushing costs up to the point where the cost savings from one-person operation were being lost.

The decision to start withdrawing the Fleetlines was taken late in 1978, barely months after the last B20s had been delivered and within five years only a handful of conventional DMSs remained in passenger service, plus the bulk of the B20s.

Operators throughout the UK and even in the Far East readily bought the London Fleetlines. In the UK they appeared in PTE, municipal, National Bus Company, Scottish Bus Group and independent fleets, where the prospect of relatively new buses to a good specification and suitable for driver-only operation was an attractive one.

Post-1984 and the creation of London Buses, the fortunes changed for the remaining DMSs. Some of the sold or disused Fleetlines returned to service and when the Bexleybus operation was set up in 1988, 14 that had been bought by Clydeside Scottish headed south again.

The change of heart came just in time to save most of the B20s, which even in the final years of the London Fleetline were to benefit from significant changes, including the fitting of Iveco engines in more than 200 of them in 1987-89.

The last Fleetline in normal service in London — DMS2438 — was withdrawn in January 1993, leaving only open-top, private hire and driver training buses in the fleet. Twenty-one were still owned when the bus companies were privatised in 1994. ■ GB

with 71 seats and space for five standing. Others were still delivered with automatic fare collection equipment and there were some with fareboxes.

Production of the Fleetline transferred from Daimler's Coventry factory to

The order for 164 double-deckers served notice to Leyland that its future business could not be taken for granted and supported MCW, which was a long-standing London supplier.

On Scania BR111DH running units, MCW mounted two-door 72-seat bodies, and they were delivered between late 1975 and early 1977 as the MD class. They were used originally with conductors on busy cross-London routes from Peckham and New Cross garages, but in 1980/81 were moved to Abbey Wood and Plumstead for driver-only operation.

They suffered corrosion problems in London as elsewhere, and there were reliability issues in their early years, leading to three being taken out of service as early as 1979. A few others fell by the wayside, but the bulk of them went with need for fleet reductions in the early 1980s, which rendered these non-standard buses surplus to requirements along with many Routemasters. All had gone by mid-1983, with some sold to other operators, including 21 for Reading Transport, which had also bought the model new.

Metro-Scania MS3 during its brief life in London. It was one of five sold to Newport Transport.
OMNIBUS SOCIETY/PETER HENSON

THE XRM

The XRM was London Transport's bus that never was, but that for a few years it hoped really would be.

If its hopes of commissioning bespoke buses withered with the fizzling out of the FRM project, they seemed to be extinguished completely by the terms of the Transport (London) Act 1969, which transferred London Transport to the Greater London Council and removed its powers to design and develop its own vehicles.

Stung by its experiences with Merlins, Swifts and Fleetlines, it made sure it regained those powers in 1975 and used them to work up some ideas for its ideal new generation double-decker, a bus unlike any being built at the time or offered since. A mock-up of such a vehicle had been around at Chiswick from the late-1960s.

This was XRM, X for Experimental, RM presumably for Routemaster. It would have eight small wheels rather than four big ones, so the floor could be made as low as possible, and in place of a conventional gearbox it would have hydraulic drive. Some of its engineers rather liked hydraulics and this was building on their use in the braking system of the Routemaster.

The engine would be in the middle, under the stair rather like on the Q Type of 40 years earlier. It believed that would provide a better balance of weight and that it would give the greatest flexibility in where the engine went. If it wanted — and it surely did — there could be a door and perhaps even a staircase at back.

That was the theory. The reality in the 1970s was that little of the technology was proven and when people started looking at the hydraulic drive it turned out to be rather fuel-inefficient. A Fleetline equipped with a prototype hydraulic drive was

slow and thirsty. With oil prices starting to climb steeply following the first of a series of Middle East crises, that was not a message the accountants wanted to hear.

Then there were the small wheels. Having eight meant that four of them would have to steer and experience with six-wheel Bedford coaches with such an arrangement was that the tyres wore more quickly.

Then there was the none-too-small matter of the engine itself. The only practical one on the market at the time was a V6 from Mercedes-Benz. Would the GLC, custodian of public money, sanction the purchase of an imported engine? Had it still been around today, that would not be an issue in a globalised automotive industry, but it was in the mid- to late-1970s.

So the design was altered. It would have four larger wheels after all, which made it less different from the increasingly reliable vehicles by then available from Leyland and MCW. There was talk of building a shorter one, mainly to take up less space in garages.

An active ride hydraulic suspension

system also was tested, initially on of all vehicles, prototype Routemaster RM1.

The intention had been to start building or commissioning the XRM in 1985 and at that point to use it to replace Titans and Metrobuses before Routemasters, perhaps concluding the project by building rear entrance XRMs to replace the Routemasters. But with the Titans and Metrobuses performing quite well, the gamble of commissioning its own design was becoming too risky.

By early 1981, before that year's game-changing GLC election, new London Transport chairman Sir Peter Masefield — a retired senior airline executive — finally took the inevitable decision that it was easier for a newcomer to implement. XRM was a bus too far. The project was dead.

Except that he did not rule out the possibility of what he called a 'Super XRM' being commissioned in another 10 years' time if more advanced propulsion systems became available. In particular — and with impressive foresight — he suggested that there would be scope for making that vehicle much lighter in order to help save fuel. ■ AM

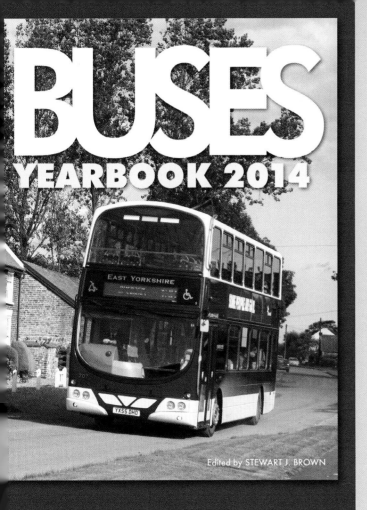

The Leyland National

L ondon Transport entered
the 1970s realising that
many of its new AEC single-
deckers would soon have to
be replaced along with its 20-year-old
RFs. Double-deckers would replace
many of the Merlins and Swifts, but it
had a continuing requirement for some
single-deckers.

The question was what should it
buy? Leyland's single-deck urban bus

was the Leyland National, conceived
in conjunction with the new National
Bus Company in the late 1960s and
replacing almost all competing models
in the Leyland family at a stroke.

This was a highly standardised
integral bus built on assembly lines at a
new factory in Workington in Cumbria
and designed for mass production.
Provided it would work on its routes,
this sounded like a new single-deck

equivalent of the big fleets of RTs and
Routemasters.

London Transport started cautiously
with a 1972 order for six 10.3m-long
two-door 36-seaters to test alongside
six of the only real alternative type on
the market, the Metro-Scania (see p81).
All 12 buses went into service late in
1973 on route S2 between Stratford
and Clapton Pond and while the Metro-
Scanias lasted in service only until 1976
the Leyland Nationals led to orders
for a further 431 of the original model
between 1975 and 1979, numbered in an
LS class.

Not every operator was happy
with the Leyland National in its first
manifestation and Leyland answered
criticisms with the National 2, which
incorporated a front-mounted radiator
and a chunkier Leyland 680 engine (and
other options) in place of the troublesome
510 unit in the original version.

London Transport bought 69
10.6m-long 28-seat National 2s in

**A Leyland National at Hampstead
Heath in July 1983.** AM

1980/81 to replace Merlins and Swifts on its prestigious Red Arrow network. As with the previous Red Arrows, these only had seats in the rear section of the bus, with standing space forward of this, though some were later re-seated as 36-seaters and 10 were rebuilt as single-door 44-seaters for the 607 route out of Uxbridge garage.

During their London lives, some Leyland Nationals were converted for use on Mobility Bus services and some were upgraded for the Docklands Shuttle service in 1989. Most had been withdrawn from normal service by 1993 although the lives of more than 40 were prolonged when it went down the National Greenway route, which involved a major rebuild by East Lancs Coachbuilders at Blackburn.

Forty-two of the Greenways were used by London General as Red Arrow buses with just 24 seats and standing space for 46. The National Greenway package was more than just a mid-life refurbishment.

Above: **One of the original six Leyland Nationals, LS2, in the white roof livery in which they were delivered.** OMNIBUS SOCIETY/PETER HENSON

A Red Arrow Leyland National 2, LS489, on Albert Embankment with Parliament across the Thames. OMNIBUS SOCIETY/ROY MARSHALL

It involved stripping the bus right down to its shell, re-panelling, new windows, new front and back ends, new engines — all with a view to giving another 10 years' useful life. The London Greenways, dating from 1981 and rebuilt in 1992-94, lasted in Red Arrow service until 2002.

Its 500-plus examples places London Transport among the largest Leyland National customers in the UK. Unlike other off-the-peg models, it seemed to manage to tame them and avoided the 'not invented here' argument that it applied to other models bought at the same time. ■ **GB**

BL93, one of the three red and yellow LHs for the Hillingdon Local Service.
OMNIBUS SOCIETY/ROY MARSHALL

The Bristol LH

The choice was limited in the mid 1970s when London Transport needed replacement single-deckers for the routes that could accommodate nothing much bigger than an RF.

Over 20 years earlier when faced with the same dilemma over its Leyland Cubs, it got Guy to develop the GS. Such a radical solution seemed out of the question this time, though maybe Bedford or Ford could have produced something to order. British Leyland was its dominant supplier and its offering in this size range was the Bristol LH.

The LH (Light Horizontal) was a mid-engined chassis introduced in 1967 with a choice of Leyland or (for a time) Perkins engines. By 1975, the only engine was the Leyland 400.

The LH was 9.1m long and there was a longer LHL variant and a shorter LHS. It was the LHS that first attracted London Transport engineers who were looking for small buses to replace the FS type Ford Transit minibuses. They borrowed examples of the LHS and front-engined Seddon Pennine Midi but plumped for the Bristol with Eastern Coach Works body. They would be its first ECW-bodied Bristols since the 190 double-deckers loaned in 1949.

The first six BS type single-door LHS6L 26-seaters entered service in 1975 and a further 11 were then ordered for 1976 delivery. The BS types were 7.3m long and 2.3m wide and like the Transits had manual gearboxes.

To replace some of the 2.3m wide RFs, it needed something narrower than the typical 2.4m or wider buses being built in the mid 1970s. Bristol could offer the narrower width and so an order for 95 LH6L with 9.1m-long ECW bodies was placed in 1974.

The first of the new BL type, single door 39-seaters, appeared early in 1976, painted red with white window surrounds, but were later painted all red. The last three entered service with yellow window surrounds for a new service in the London Borough of Hillingdon. Unlike most other LHs, they had automatic transmission and ECW modified the bodywork to have more but shallower steps than on those for other customers.

The smaller BS types had fairly short lives in service and were withdrawn by 1981, finding new homes around the country. BLs took their place.

The BLs lasted longer, in spite of route withdrawals and the introduction of larger buses on some of their routes, and although the first examples were sold in 1982, some survived in service until 1994 and some even longer as driver trainers. Many were sold for further service, notably to Guernseybus, where the restricted dimensions suited the island's road system. ■ GB

LHS BS1 on route C11 linking Archway Station and Willesden Green.
OMNIBUS SOCIETY/PETER HENSON

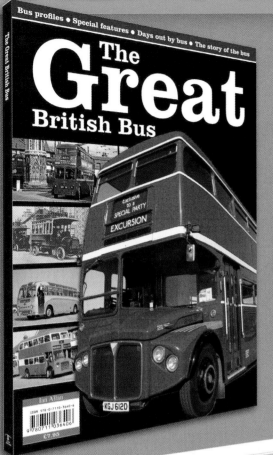

Titan, Metrobus &Olympian

T474 in Parliament Square in September 1987. It was
new in 1982 and latterly was with Stagecoach in London,
transferring to one of its Sussex fleets in 1995. GB

After its disastrous vehicle buying in the 1960s and 1970s, London Transport must have hoped that things would get better. And as the 1970s ended, they did.

With more than half an eye on London orders, Leyland was developing what it hoped would be its all-purpose double-deck, replacing the Atlantean, Fleetline and Bristol VRT models. Operators had bought the integral Leyland National single-decker, so it reasoned that they would also buy an advanced integral double-decker.

As it turned out, they were wrong, but in the meantime Metro-Cammell Weymann, which had been primarily a large-volume bodybuilder, had seen the single-deck body market decline because of the Leyland National and feared the same could happen when the new double-decker came on stream.

Having developed the single-deck Metro-Scania and double-deck Metropolitan with Scania, MCW decided it was time to develop its own complete double-decker. This materialised as the Metrobus in 1978, but not before Leyland had launched its advanced Titan.

The Titan bristled with the sort of features that got London Transport engineers excited — integral construction, independent front suspension, hydraulic brakes — and with an attractive body developed by Park Royal, also part of the British Leyland family, it was impressive.

The trouble was, most other operators did not agree that the Titan was the panacea for their 1980s orders, and the Titan's reputation was not helped by delays getting it into production and then the decision to switch production from Park Royal to Workington. Most operators who had been persuaded to place orders quickly cancelled them and apart from small batches for Greater Manchester and West Midlands PTEs and Reading Buses, the Titan became a strictly London model with 1,125 supplied new between 1978 and 1984 and classed T.

The Metrobus had fewer whistles and bells, but had the engineers' favourite Gardner 6LXB engine — as did most London Titans — although some Metrobuses were fitted with Cummins L10 engines and others in later life with Gardner's 6XLDT.

Metrobus M628 was new in 1981 and remained in London service with Arriva until 2001. OMNIBUS SOCIETY/ROY MARSHALL

M1365 at Victoria in July 1995 in the livery of MTL London Northern, which sold the business to Metroline in 1997. This bus, new in October 1985, remained in service until February 2003. AM

One of the two Metrobus MkIIs bought as part of the vehicle evaluation programme, M1441. OMNIBUS SOCIETY/ROY MARSHALL

ECW-bodied Arriva Leyland Olympian L201 passing St Martin's-in-the-Fields in July 2002. GB

It found favour with a wider circle of operators than the Titan, including all of the PTEs and some municipal and state-owned operators. London bought 1,440 of the original model plus 29 of the simpler MkII, and it acquired second-hand versions from three English PTEs, just as it had bought the five West Midlands PTE Titans. They were all classed M.

The first Metrobuses and Titans were delivered to London Transport within months of each other in 1978. It had already inspected prototypes of both types and had placed initial orders for 50 of each.

Over the next few years the orders see-sawed between Leyland and MCW, sometimes reflecting the production difficulties that Leyland was experiencing, but they worked pretty well out of the box and became a major part of

the bus fleet in the 1980s, the last examples surviving into the 21st century.

The original Metrobus picked up design features from the Metropolitan, notably the asymmetrical front windscreen layout with a slightly deeper nearside screen. They were 9.6m long and 2.5m wide. The majority had 71-seat two-door bodies with lower deck space for 20 standees, but there were 16 examples new in 1980 with the lower deck seating reduced to just nine with extensive racking for luggage for the Airbus services between central London and Heathrow Airport.

New Airbus Metrobuses arrived in 1984, with high-backed coach seats and a total capacity of just 50, again with just nine seats on the lower deck; they also had lifts at the centre door to help passengers with disabilities and anchor points for two wheelchairs. Some older

Metrobuses were converted to a similar layout, but without the facilities for disabled passengers, and these were available as relief Airbus vehicles for heavy summer loadings.

Twenty-two 1984 Metrobuses received Cummins L10 engines, a type that would become very familiar in Britain, and one was retro-fitted with a Deutz air-cooled engine between 1985 and 1990. The original hydraulic brakes on the Metrobus fleet were replaced by more conventional air brakes in the late 1980s.

In later life some were converted to single door layout and others received high-back coach seats for private hire work.

The introduction of route tendering sometimes led to a need for additional buses and London Buses, as it was now named, bought single-door Metrobuses from Busways Travel, Greater Manchester and Yorkshire Rider. Two of the Yorkshire Rider examples had Alexander bodies, for although the majority of Metrobuses built carried MCW bodies, underframes were also available with Alexander or Northern Counties bodies.

As part of its Alternative Vehicle Examination trials (see p92), in 1983 London Transport ordered 12 examples of current double-deck models to test in service, including three Metrobuses.

Two MkII Metrobuses arrived, but a third to a radical new specification never materialised. A further 29 examples arrived in 1987/88, on a short-term lease for the new Harrow Buses network and wore a light red and cream livery.

First Titans

The first production Titans went into service late in 1978 and delivery of the first 250, assembled at the Park Royal factory in London, was completed by July 1980. Then, with the closure of Park Royal and the eventual transfer of production to Workington, deliveries recommenced early in 1981 with regular supplies to London until T1125 arrived late in 1984.

The standard London Titan had a Gardner 6LXB engine, but a small number had Leyland's L11 or TL11 engines. The 9.6m long by 2.5m wide two-door bodies had various internal layouts, with seats for 66, 68 or 70 passengers.

Most were delivered in all-red livery, although some early examples had white upper deck window surrounds and after

Still in original condition with white top deck window surrounds in September 1982 is Park Royal-built Titan T6 at Hornchurch. TONY WILSON

privatisation, some carried their new owners' variations on London red with additional colours or stripes.

The Olympian was Leyland's natural successor to the Titan, a chassis produced in response to the negative reaction among many operators towards the Titan and sold widely outside London. Three with Eastern Coach Works bodies (L1 to L3) were bought for

the Alternative Vehicle Examination trials and 260 followed with Gardner 6LXB engines, Hydracyclic gearboxes and two-door ECW 68-seat two-door bodies — some with high-back coach-type seats for express services and private hires.

These turned out to be the last buses bodied by ECW, as the Lowestoft factory was closed after the last of the London

bodies was completed. They entered service in 1986/87 and were concentrated in south and south-east London.

The 10 Olympians with high-back seats were bought for the X68 and 177 Express routes, and the last four, from what would become the Selkent fleet, later received registrations from Routemasters and the names *Renown, Buccaneer, Invincible* and *Conqueror*.

Given the freedom to choose their own buses, the London Buses companies and their privatised successors, as well as the firms that won London contracts, bought substantial fleets of Leyland and Volvo Olympians, with bodies by Alexander, Leyland, Optare and Northern Counties, right through to the end of Olympian production and the switch to low-floor double-deckers.

In that initial round of sales of the London Buses companies to the private sector, there were Metrobuses in most fleets, except London Central, East London, Selkent and Westlink, where the majority of Titans could be found, reflecting the practice of creating separate Metrobus and Titan garages.

Of the 5,000-plus buses involved in the sales, the Metrobuses and Titans accounted for over 2,000, with 1,420 Metrobuses and 752 Titans – withdrawals had started in 1992, with many readily finding new homes. ■ **GB**

The Harrow Buses Metrobus MkII fleet operated in a livery with no obvious London Buses parentage, as shown by M1471 at Wealdstone. Most moved on to new owners in 1992 after the Harrow routes were retendered and all 29 were returned to the leasing company. TONY WILSON

New colours, new owners

Buses of many colours and shapes swept into London as competitive tendering broke the old London Transport monopoly and further change saw the red bus operation divided into smaller units and privatised

The first of London Buses' new local network operations was Roundabout, serving the Orpington area with maroon and grey minibuses like RH8, one of 24 Robin Hood-bodied Iveco Daily 49-10s. OMNIBUS SOCIETY/ROY MARSHALL

When London Regional Transport — it soon reverted to calling itself London Transport — took over in June 1984, some changes to the bus operation were already becoming apparent.

One was the Alternative Vehicle Evaluation (AVE) trial to find the best successors to the Leyland Titan and MCW Metrobus. Twelve buses were ordered but only 11 delivered: three Leyland Olympians, two MCW Metrobus MkII, three Dennis Dominator and three Volvo Ailsa. These were closer to the standard of buses built for other operators, but still with features tailored for London operation.

H3, one of the three Northern Counties-bodied Dennis Dominators, in Parliament Square. It is following a Routemaster with logo for Selkent District. The H in the fleetnumber was for Hestair, Dennis's parent company in 1984. OMNIBUS SOCIETY/ROY MARSHALL

An order followed for 260 ECW-bodied Leyland Olympians, the last bulk double-deck contract placed by London Transport, which also was taking another look at the finer points of bus design, seeking improvements in passenger flow as once again — with the GLC removed from its life — driver-only operation was on the agenda.

It asked Ogle Design, then a leading consultancy working in the automotive industry, to develop a bus for the 1990s. Ogle looked at what made open rear platform buses work so well on busy London routes, concluding that it was passengers having the ability to approach them from a wide angle and not just through the slot of a doorway entirely on the side.

Its solution, reached after volunteers spent hours climbing on and off wooden platforms simulating different shapes of bus door, was for the front corner of the bus to open up in a reverse image of an open back. It also concluded that straight staircases — as used in prewar London buses — were better than curved ones and recommended lower steps to benefit people with impaired mobility.

The beginnings of a new specification bus were indeed being seen and the Olympians incorporated some of them, but changes to the organisation of London Transport and its bus routes delayed other innovations for a quarter century.

Competitive tendering

Those changes started with the legislation that created London Regional Transport, as this stipulated that it create subsidiary companies, London Buses and London Underground, to operate its services and offer other operators the chance of providing its services by competitive tender.

The new companies started trading in April 1985 by which time the first routes had gone out to tender, with contracts awarded to start in spring 1985.

The first tendering round involved 12 routes and in an extraordinarily neat outcome, London Buses retained six, while four of the others went to National Bus Company subsidiaries (two each to Eastern National and London Country), the other two to independent companies (London Buslines and Crystals of Orpington). The old Country Area was apparently winning another little victory over its estranged red bus cousins.

London Buslines, set up by coach operator Len Wright, did what several

Ogle's mock-up of its ideal London double-decker, with split-level front platform and cutaway corner to improve accessibility. LONDON TRANSPORT

London Country's success in winning tendered services saw it purchase 63 secondhand Leyland Atlanteans in 1985/86. Thirty-two with Alexander bodies and panoramic windows came from Strathclyde Transport. One of these, AN332, shows how London Transport's destination information was squeezed into the space provided when new in Glasgow in 1974. OMNIBUS SOCIETY/PETER HENSON

other successful tenderers would over the next year or so: buy discarded ex-London Transport DMS Fleetlines.

The tendering system allowed — encouraged even — new operators to paint their London buses in their own colours, so Eastern National's and London Country's were green, London Buslines' were yellow and Crystals' cream and blue. They displayed stickers with London Regional Transport bulls-eye roundels.

They also had to display their route number on the back, which on many of the tenderers' buses in the early years was in white on a black board without any

illumination after dark. Most had one door while London Buses ran mainly two-door buses.

This pattern continued, with selected routes offered for tender and a mix of private and public sector operators winning the contracts. London Country was particularly successful, as it had garages scattered around the outskirts of London, leading it to acquire surplus double-deckers from elsewhere in the National Bus Company as well as other operators.

A highlight in 1988 was when route 24 became the first major one in central

Other than a new modern fleetname and a narrow orange line separating red from the grey skirt, London General livery after privatisation was largely unaltered. ML1, leaving Putney Bridge station for Tolworth, was the first of 15 Marshall Minibus 29-seaters. The low-floor Minibus, a rival for the hugely successful Dennis Dart and built in Cambridge, was a rare beast. Only 48 were built, 32 of them for London. A much greater number of similar Marshall-bodied low-floor Darts operated in London. AM

London to go to a private operator, Grey-Green, whose green, grey and orange Volvo Citybuses began traversing Whitehall and Parliament Square that November.

By then, the National Bus Company's subsidiaries had been privatised. London Country was split into four separate companies in 1986, ready for sale. Their new owners continued to win London contracts, although they also faced huge challenges from competitors on their home patches and had to cut costs.

Smaller units

As it started losing bigger chunks of its business to competitors, London Buses set up lower cost units to bid to retain more work, placing it sometimes in conflict with its drivers' trade union when terms and conditions were changed. Keeping or reacquiring depreciated DMS Fleetlines also appeared to make it more competitive.

Some of these units had completely different identities. Roundabout, with maroon and grey minibuses, began operating in Orpington in August 1986. Harrow Buses in November 1987 and Bexleybus in January 1988, with a mix of new and secondhand buses and liveries of red and cream at Harrow Buses, blue and cream at Bexleybus.

The Harrow fleet had new leased

Metrobus MkIIs and secondhand Volvo Ailsas, while Bexleybus had new leased Olympians and older Leyland Titans, Leyland Nationals and DMS Fleetlines. The iconic red London bus was beginning to look like an endangered species.

Even some of the red buses were not what they would have been a few years before: secondhand Ailsas and Metrobuses with one door instead of two.

More change followed. Bus services outside London had been deregulated in October 1986, allowing operators to compete with each other, and there was pressure for this to be extended to London or at least its outer suburbs.

In preparation for such possible change, London Buses was restructured with 12 subsidiary companies managing different parts of the network from April 1989. This took forward a process begun in December 1979 when many day-to-day operations were devolved to districts, each with its own logo.

From west round clockwise to south-west London, 11 of the new companies were CentreWest, Metroline, London Northern, Leaside Buses, London Forest, East London, Selkent, London Central, South London, London General and London United. Selkent was an abbreviation of South East London & Kent, while London Central, London

General and London United revived pre-London Transport names.

The 12th company was London Coaches, operating sightseeing tours and other commercial work and which had operated express coaches linking London with Birmingham and Eastbourne in 1986-88. There also was Westlink, a 60-bus unit in south-west London set up to bid for tendered work. London Forest lasted only until 1991, closed after a tender win went wrong, its operations split between East London and Leaside.

Managing directors of the new companies came from within and outside London Buses. Among them, at CentreWest, was Peter Hendy, one of London Transport's graduate recruits from the 1970s, today London's transport commissioner and knighted in January 2013.

New bus types

Following delivery of the 260 Leyland Olympians, the emphasis at London Buses switched to mini and midibuses, based on van and light truck chassis to begin with, later on smaller bus designs. These included the stylish Optare CityPacer on Volkswagen chassis for some Roundabout routes and a high frequency service between Camden and Oxford Circus.

CentreWest bought Alexander-bodied

Mercedes-Benz 28-seaters to increase frequencies and replace Routemasters on routes 28 (Golders Green-Wandsworth) and 31 (Camden Town-Chelsea), the last Routemaster routes that did not penetrate central London. They were branded Gold Arrow. Their introduction helped attract new drivers put off handling larger vehicles.

Later in 1989 the Dennis Dart became available, a small lightweight rear-engined bus with the layout of a bigger vehicle. London Buses was one of its first customers and these were the first of thousands for London alone. If there was a standard London bus of the early 1990s, it was a Dart with Plaxton Pointer or Wright Handybus body.

There were some new double-deckers, too, mostly for specific contracts. Many were built to the manufacturers' own specification and had just one door, but by 1992 things were returning a little closer to the old pattern, with 40 two-door Alexander-bodied Leyland Olympians for Leaside.

There also was a brief renewed attempt at running bigger single-deckers — Dennis Lances at Selkent and Metroline, Volvo B10Bs at London General.

The other tendered service operators purchased a variety of vehicles for specific contracts, more often than not with one door and in the case of double-deckers usually of lower overall height so they could have a second life in places where bridges and other obstacles are a problem.

While operators could still paint their buses more or less as they chose, the tendered bus unit tightened up other standards, especially the clarity and consistency of destination displays. The black boards of the early days were no longer acceptable.

In 1993, two Routemaster routes were awarded to non-London Buses operators. Kentish Bus (formerly London Country South East) took over the 19 and BTS (formerly Borehamwood Travel Services) the 13. London Buses leased the buses to them and allowed them to paint them in their own liveries rather than London red.

Privatisation

Plans to deregulate London's buses were dropped in 1993, but the London Buses subsidiaries were privatised in 1994. London Coaches had been sold to its managers in 1992. Westlink went to its managers in January 1994; they sold it on to new owners within three months.

CentreWest, Metroline, London General

and London United all were bought by their managers and employees, London Northern by MTL (the privatised Merseyside Transport), Leaside and South London by Cowie (now called Arriva) which owned Grey-Green, East London and Selkent by Stagecoach and London Central by Go-Ahead Group. There have been several subsequent changes of ownership.

Allowing new operators to stamp their multi-coloured identities on their buses may have demonstrated the results of competitive tendering, but London Transport and the government were keen to ensure that privatisation did not eliminate the red London bus. They stipulated that at least on routes penetrating central London, 80% of the paintwork should be London red, regardless of whether the bus was owned by a former London Buses company or one of the newcomers.

The 10 big companies complemented London red with colours of their own choice. Most were subtle, with grey or white added. Cowie applied diagonal yellow stripes toward the back of some of its buses. Metroline added dark blue. London United grey roofs and top deck

windows. All gave prominence to their fleetnames and logos.

Their choices of new vehicles became more varied, though for double-deckers most bought Volvo Olympians with Alexander or Northern Counties bodies. They exercised more choice over how they were specified and Stagecoach made a point of buying lowheight double-deckers, which it could move to other parts of the country after their first tough years in London, though most had two doors for London.

As described on p98, low-floor buses arrived in 1994, revolutionising accessibility and introducing standards for all operators to meet on tendered services.

The same year, London Transport secured powers for Croydon Tramlink, using modern low-floor articulated trams on a combination of former heavy rail lines, new track and town centre street running to connect Croydon with Wimbledon and Beckenham Junction from May 2000. Feeder buses complemented this return of trams after 48 years.

More change came with local government changes in 2000. London Regional Transport was about to disappear. ■ AM

London Coaches acquired six new 70-seat double-deck coaches to operate new longer distance express services in 1986/87. LC1 was one of a pair of Leyland Olympians with East Lancs body for an Eastbourne route. Four six-wheel MCW Metroliners helped operate a London Liner service to Birmingham. OMNIBUS SOCIETY/ ROY MARSHALL

Each of the new London Buses subsidiaries carried its own fleetname as well as the London Buses bulls-eye roundel. This is Metroline DR95, a Dennis Dart with 28-seat Plaxton Pointer body. Privatisation saw Metroline change the grey skirt colour to dark blue. AM

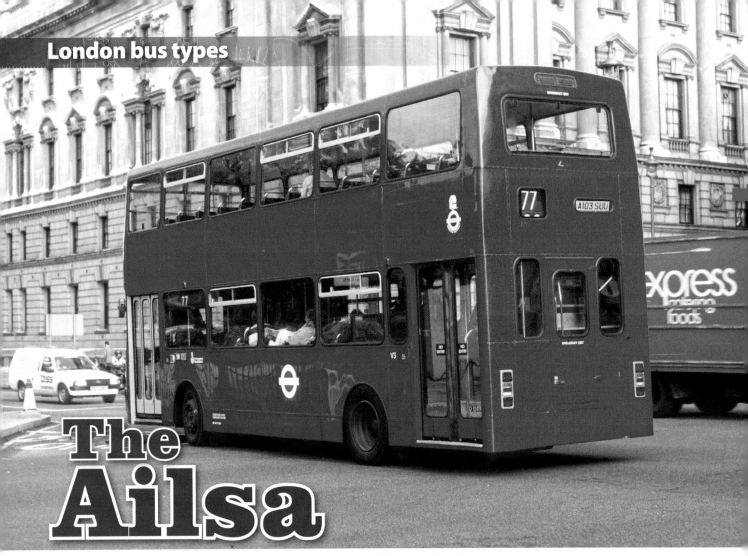

The Ailsa

V3 on trial on route 77A. Its twin-stair layout anticipated the New Bus for London by 27 years. OMNIBUS SOCIETY/ROY MARSHALL

Given that it bought Routemasters until 1968 and was one of the last British operators to buy rear platform buses with front engines, it is perhaps surprising that it took London Transport so long to buy the Volvo Ailsa — and doubly surprising that it then bought so many secondhand.

The Ailsa, built in Scotland from 1973 and designed in Britain, was a response to the bus industry's problems with early rear-engined double-deckers like the Leyland Atlantean and Daimler Fleetline. It combined the layout of a rear-engined bus — front wheels behind the door, next to the driver — with a front engine.

This was a very compact engine — 6.7litre when the rear-engine buses had something nearer 11litre — turbocharged to deliver a lot of power.

It also delivered a lot of noise and it was hardly what might be called sophisticated, certainly not by comparison with the Scania-powered MCW Metropolitan launched at the same time. But it was robust and

reasonably reliable, and because there was no engine at the back, it would be possible to have a rear door if an operator wanted that.

The Ailsa sold modestly to a few customers and was about to go out of production when London Buses included three of them in its 1984 Alternative Vehicle Evaluation programme, all with the first Alexander bodies ever built for London Transport.

V1 and V2 were fairly conventional by Ailsa standards, 78-seat two-door buses with a staircase at the front and the second door directly behind the front wheels. Like all Ailsas, they had a three-piece front door designed to fold around the space left by the engine on the front platform.

V3 was something else, with two staircases, one at the front and one at the back, where the second door was located. The idea was that this could be operated with or without a conductor. It was hoped that in driver-only mode that passengers would exit by the rear door, but a blindspot prevented it from working without a conductor. In that mode of operation, it could theoretically be a new age

Above: **One of the Alexander-bodied West Midlands Ailsas, V30, in August 1987, shortly after entering service at Potters Bar.** TONY WILSON

Below: **Most of the trial buses operated on route 170 from Stockwell garage. This is V2 at Charing Cross.** OMNIBUS SOCIETY/ROY MARSHALL

Routemaster, with passengers hopping on and off the back platform.

Being the only one of its kind probably did not help and after just two years, V3 had the rear door removed (it kept both staircases) and was moved to Potters Bar along with the other two and used as a driver-only bus.

That is when the story became even more surprising. London Buses was on a secondhand bus-buying spree in 1987 that added 62 more Ailsas new around 1976/77. A dozen (V4 to V15) were South Yorkshire PTE buses with two-door Van Hool-McArdle bodies built in Ireland. The other 50 (V16 to V65) were an entire batch from West Midlands PTE with an older style of one-door Alexander body.

All the South Yorkshire and 22 of the West Midlands ones also went to Potters Bar, the other 28 to Harrow Buses. They were all out of the fleet again after three years. V3 lasted until 1992 when it overturned, but it was rescued for preservation and restoration to unique original condition. V1 and V2 left in 1995. ■ **AM**

The low-floor revolution

ANDREW BRADDOCK tells the inside story of one of the biggest recent improvements in bus travel in London — the development and introduction of low-floor vehicles

In my second period of working for London Transport from 1991, I was responsible for ensuring that bus and rail services took account of the needs of disabled people and

I suppose my main qualification for this task was the experience of running a few wheelchair-accessible Leyland Nationals at Alder Valley, which my predecessor as

traffic manager there had developed as a specialised adjunct to the company's private hire business.

Some of these vehicles were subsequently used on CareLine, the UK's first scheduled bus service with access for wheelchair-users but open to all, which Alder Valley North (later The Bee Line) ran between Heathrow Airport and

central London with some Department of Transport funding.

I also served on the National Bus Company's working group — chaired by the late Claudia Flanders — charged with meeting the needs of disabled people. Claudia was the widow of Michael Flanders, of Flanders & Swann fame — creators of the splendid 'Big six-wheeler scarlet painted London Transport Diesel-engined 97-horsepower Om-ni-bus' — who had been a wheelchair-user for most of his life.

As an American, Claudia was well aware that during the 1970s it became common

One of the Wright Pathfinder-bodied Scanias operated by Stagecoach on the 101, showing wheelchair access by the centre door and the 'zip effect' arrow graphics imported from Dortmund. ANDREW BRADDOCK

Above: **Life before low-floor. In 1992, a mother holds her toddler in her left arm and a folded buggy in the right as they prepare to board a London & Country Volvo Citybus in Carshalton. The Citybus has an underfloor engine and three steps in the entrance.** AM

Right: **With low-floor, this mother can wheel child and buggy straight on to the step-free front of the bus.** AB

in the United States for the then standard types of high-floor city buses to be fitted with lifts so that wheelchair-users could board and alight, in response to growing pressure for disabled people to be given access to public transport. This led to federal legislation mandating wheelchair access to bus and rail services.

Chained to Routemasters
During my first few weeks back at 55 Broadway, I met a lot of aggrieved wheelchair-users who often chained themselves to Routemasters on the service 9 stand at Aldwych (much to the delight of the crews, who simply drank more tea while missing a round trip), and they clearly believed that their rights should take precedence over operational practicality, and the convenience of other passengers, by calling on London Transport to follow American practice.

Fortunately, there was some experience with enabling disabled Londoners to travel on regular timetabled services as the first Mobility Bus had taken to the streets in 1984. This also involved our old friend

the Leyland National, this time with a platform lift at door two.

Eligible disabled people could also use the pre-booked Dial-a-Ride minibus service, initially funded by the London Boroughs but a London Transport responsibility from 1986 (these too were operated with high-floor, lift-equipped vehicles), and they could have a Taxicard to make use of the growing number of wheelchair-accessible London black cabs.

Mobility Bus represented an overlaid network of routes, operated in addition to conventional bus services — though at best each one ran on only two days a week with two journeys in each direction. As these services really only provided for short local trips and both Taxicard and Dial-a-Ride were subject to trip limits, the mobility of the users was restricted.

The experience with Mobility Bus (and CareLine, which had become a London Transport responsibility with National Bus Company privatisation) amply demonstrated that use of lifts to provide wheelchair access was a time-consuming process, and for the intensive bus system

in London (and other major European cities) a time of four or more minutes to board one wheelchair-user (with a similar alighting time further along the route) would have caused unacceptable delays to the services and to other passengers.

The low-floor concept, however, coupled with the use of powered ramps and rear-facing wheelchair spaces featuring an 'ironing board' backrest, provided a solution to wheelchair-user boarding and alighting that took less than 1min (with practice) and this was to emerge as London's preferred option to cope with the not unreasonable demands for people in wheelchairs to be given access to bus services.

A German invention
Low-floor buses were developed in Germany in the late 1970s, initially as airport transfer buses, which are significantly wider than normal. The low-floor layout made entering and exiting with luggage much easier, and by 1977 Neoplan had built its first low-floor bus for use on scheduled urban services.

The other major German manufacturers (MAN, Mercedes-Benz and Setra) quickly followed suit.

As a result of having no steps at the doorways, these vehicles were quicker and safer for ambulant passengers to get on or off but as yet did not have any wheelchair access. In 1986, Munich became the first city to add a wheelchair ramp to its low-floor buses and this feature rapidly became widespread in Germany and in several other countries as the concept spread.

The London Low-floor Bus Project was set up in 1992 and the Department for Transport decided sponsored a parallel introduction of low-floor buses on a route in North Tyneside.

In London, five routes were selected involving five of the bus companies then owned by London Buses (and privatised in 1994):

■ East London 101: North Woolwich-Wanstead (Upton Park Garage)
■ London United 120: Hounslow-Northolt (Hounslow Garage)
■ Leaside 144: Edmonton-Muswell Hill (Wood Green Garage)
■ Metroline 186: Brent Cross-Northwick Park (Harrow Weald Garage)
■ CentreWest 222: Hounslow-Uxbridge (Uxbridge Garage)

I was keen to ensure that the experience gained with significant numbers of low-floor buses in Germany should be passed on to my colleagues in the five London companies so we set up a series of study tours to Aachen, Düsseldorf, Essen, Hamburg and Kassel during 1993.

Mixed groups of operating and engineering staff, including trade union representatives, participated and a very useful knowledge transfer took place. Through the contacts made, each of the operators was twinned with a German city in the Low-floor Bus Partnership or *Niederflurbus Partnerschaft*. The city of Dortmund was also involved, kindly agreeing that we could copy its 'zip effect' vertical stripe with a broad arrow-head pointing to the low level of the bus floor.

Once the number of buses required was calculated, discussions began with potential manufacturers and for some time it looked as though a right-hand-drive adaptation of one or more continental vehicles would be selected, with Dutch Berkhof bodywork on an MAN chassis (one such vehicle came to the UK as a demonstrator) and the Belgian Van Hool A300 integral as front-runners, but in time a combination of Wright bodywork with both Dennis and Scania chassis emerged with an acceptable package.

Sixty-eight were ordered from Dennis (38 Lance SLF chassis) and Scania (30 N113CRL), all with the Northern Irish business's new Pathfinder body. When built in 1993/94 they were about 25% more expensive than the same size of conventional single-deck bus, but within three years the price premium had fallen to around 5%.

In many ways these vehicles were more like typical continental buses than previous single-deckers built for London. They were fitted, for example, with swing-plug doors and a German-made Bode powered ramp at door two and had London's first power-driven roller-blind destination displays.

The initial route (120) was converted in January 1994 and the other four followed during the year. The success of these buses resulted in the concept being extended and by 1996 Dennis had designed a low-floor version of the popular Dart midibus and over the next few years DAF, Dennis, Scania and Volvo were all producing low-floor double-deckers.

Dramatic improvements

Though the introduction of low-floor buses was geared to meeting the needs of disabled people, they dramatically improved the public transport offer for millions of others — especially those travelling with small children, heavy baggage or shopping.

Older passengers particularly benefit from the step-free doorways and kneeling suspension. Passenger numbers in London and elsewhere increased with the change to low-floor buses, so these accessible vehicles made good business sense too.

Now, throughout the UK, the bus industry is well on the way to achieving the goal of a fully-accessible bus system,

A wheelchair user parks herself safely behind a padded 'ironing board' between front wheel and centre door, alongside three tip-up seats available for other passengers when no wheelchairs or buggies were aboard. Tip-ups proved less than robust and are no longer fitted in London buses. AB

which the Public Service Vehicles Accessibility Regulations require to be in place by 1 January 2016 (2017 for double-deckers; 2020 for coaches) and the London fleet has been compliant since the end of 2005.

I was always proud of the way in which most of the drivers on the five initial low-floor routes quickly became accustomed to having wheelchair-users travel on their bus, and in my frequent journeying around the capital it is now commonplace to see what we pioneered 20 years ago being an accepted fact.

What makes it work so well is the simple access to and from the wheelchair space at door two and, from a difficult start, the reliability of the ramps that bridge the gap to the kerb at stops.

From the introduction of the first horse-drawn buses in 1826, through the opening of the initial section of the Underground in 1863 and the inauguration of the city's electric tramway network in 1901, and right up to the 1980s little or no thought was given to the needs of passengers with reduced mobility.

Yet among London's population of almost 8million there are more than 1million older people and a similar number with a disability that makes it difficult or impossible to use public transport. Low-floor buses have made a huge difference to those two million and I firmly believe that a public transport system accessible to all is a mark of a civilised society. ■

Exclusive reader offer

Limited Edition Bus Model Pack

Key Publishing have teamed up with Exclusive First Editions to produce a superb set of three 1/76 scale bus models exclusively for readers of The London Bus. All models feature authentic new routes and destinations and are sure to sell out very quickly.

Production has been strictly limited to just 200 sets which are priced at just £61.90 plus postage and packing. This represents a huge saving on our normally priced limited edition models.

£61.90
+P&P

Each model set includes a numbered certificate of authenticity. The price includes postage within the UK (Overseas postage is available on request). Don't miss out on what is sure to become one of the most sought-after model bus offers of the year!

AUTHENTIC NEW ROUTES AND DESTINATIONS

JUST 200 SETS AVAILABLE!

Great Yarmouth Transport Liveried Routemaster, RML2717

Brighton & Hove, Thomas Tilling Liveried RML Routemaster

Kentish Bus Liveried Leyland Atlantian

Exclusive First Editions

First Eastern Counties operate three former London Routemasters on its Great Yarmouth Route 3 service. The buses all wear liveries representing the three constituent operators of Great Yarmouth that combined to form the present First operation. Our model represents RML2717 which sports the blue and cream of Great Yarmouth Transport operating on Route 8 to Caister.

Brighton & Hove has combined its own heritage with that of 72-seat Routemaster RML2317 by painting it in the red, cream and grey livery of Thomas Tilling, the London based predecessor of Brighton Hove & District. The vehicle is used on a number of services including the special events day 472 service between Brighton and East Grinstead Station on the Bluebell Railway.

Throughout the 1990s until early in 2002, Kentish Bus operated a fleet of Optare bodied Leyland Olympians. Our model represents vehicle No. 754 in the attractive Kentish Bus livery which has only ever been produced by Buses magazine in model form on this type of vehicle. Our model depicts the Olympian working Route 422 between Bexleyheath and North Greenwich.

TO ORDER: CALL Key Direct on +44(0)1780 480404 BUSES

London by bus

One of First's Eclipse Gemini 2-bodied Volvos heading east with the Gherkin building behind.

Route 25

An Enviro400 and the 'giant kisses' artwork in Stratford.

The 25 is a route of two parts. In central London it serves Oxford Street, Holborn and the City, making often slow, patient progress past some of the best-known landmarks: Centre Point, Holborn, St Paul's Cathedral, the Bank of England.

Beyond the City, it becomes a 'main drag' route, following a long, straight and almost unswerving path to the east and slightly to the north, ending up in Ilford.

It's a seriously busy route, requiring nearly 60 buses in all. There often seems barely a minute between them, yet at peak times they're so full that there may not be any space for you on the first one that arrives.

For more than six years articulated buses operated it, but following Transport for London's rethink on that subject, double-deckers were reinstated in 2011. As we write this, the route is operated by First London, using immaculate Volvo B9TLs with Wright Eclipse Gemini 2 bodywork, plus the occasional

London by bus

An equestrian statue in memory of Prince Albert at Holborn Circus.

Alexander Dennis Enviro400. But First has sold its Lea Interchange activities to an Australian-owned business, Tower Transit, which was due to take over the current contract in June 2013.

Heading east, the 25 starts out from Oxford Circus, so you'll only find it in the eastern half of Oxford Street. Then it has to negotiate the often-slow Crossrail road works around Holborn Underground, finally emerging in Holborn itself, where it passes the redbrick Gothic Holborn Bars, the traditional home of the Prudential (now a conference venue) and crosses Holborn Viaduct.

Many of the buses arriving from Ilford turn short here, at City Thameslink station or at St Paul's, avoiding the time-consuming extension to Oxford Circus.

On through a succession of historic City streets — Cheapside, Poultry, Cornhill, Leadenhall Street, all with their curious mix of traditional and ultra-modern architecture.

Then we turn north-east, and as if at the flick of switch the scenery and atmosphere change completely. We're in Whitechapel High Street, a place of street markets, traditional low-rise Victorian architecture and a diverse mix of cultures, accents and languages.

Whitechapel Road takes over, then Mile End Road, and we pass through a succession of east London districts: Whitechapel, Stepney Green, Mile End, Bow Road — all with their stations on the Underground. Mile End is one of the busiest, featuring a major road junction crossed by a remarkable overbridge. This gives passage to a footpath linking parks on either side, complete with shrubs masking joggers and dog-walkers from the tumult of traffic below.

At Bow, the landscape opens out as a flyover takes the main road across the junction above the multi-lane Blackwall

Tunnel Approach, largely hidden in an underpass. On the other side, the architecture abruptly grows grander and multi-coloured skyscrapers loom; it feels as if we're entering a city within a city.

It's Stratford, the jewel in the Borough of Newham's crown: already trendy even before the Olympics, and now permanently on the tourist map, thanks in part to the giant Westfield shopping centre and gleaming office developments. Here we dive off into a thronging bus station, adjacent to the tube station and Docklands Light Railway terminus and not far from the main Olympic stadium. It's overlooked by a strange abstract montage of blue-green diamond mouldings on poles — a bit like giant kisses floating in the air.

The older part of Stratford centre is impressive too. Eastbound, a buses-only lane takes us against the one-way traffic in the Broadway, a wide thoroughfare with a backdrop of offices and civic

buildings in an impressive array of Victorian styles. Facing them on the other side, a 1970s shopping centre competes as best it can with its more modern rival.

Eastwards out of Stratford on Romford Road, the surroundings retain an elegant air as we pass the University of East London campus. Then we progress through a further succession of bustling East London communities: Forest Gate, Manor Park (where some buses on route 25 turn short), Woodgrange Park. There are more little gems of Victorian architecture here — the old Manor Park Library, for instance — though the area seems to be waiting to benefit from the halo effect of Stratford's regeneration.

Then we break out of this environment to pass under the North Circular Road, which at this point is a modern six-lane flyover; and on the other side everything changes again. We're back in the land of high-rise offices, and at the top of a short incline we're pitched straight into the centre of Ilford.

This feels truly like self-contained town. Victorian, 1960s and modern buildings vie for attention and there's a proper high street (actually it's called High Road). Some of the buses on the 25 do a circuit of the town centre and pick up here, while others congregate in the modern bus turn-around in Chapel Road. Then it's back into London; but at busy times, don't expect to get there in under an hour and half. ■ **PR**

An eastbound 25 leaves Stratford bus station.

80 years of capital service 103

A story of success

The history of London's buses over the past 13 years has been one of steady growth in passenger numbers and the development of a service supported by the political commitment of two elected mayors

The story of the London bus since 2000 is of an extraordinary renaissance, as inspirational as the first years of London Transport from its formation in 1933. Something that the bus managers of 55 years ago would have found hard to believe could ever happen as they wrestled with declining demand, rising car ownership and the damaging effects of the 1958 strike.

Today, for all its wealth, London — especially its inner areas — has lower levels of car ownership and use than most of the rest of the UK. Growing numbers of London households have no car and for many that is a lifestyle choice. They do not need one, as the public transport system is so comprehensive and easy to use.

Thanks also to a continuing rise in the London population — 8.7million within the 32 boroughs in 2011, up 12% on 10 years earlier, and projected to top 9million by 2021 — the number of people using buses has also grown.

The total for 2012/13 is 2.3billion passengers a year, up 60% since 2000 and 28% since 2004/05. That is higher than in any year since 1960 and is above the bus and trolleybus figure for 1958 when the strike helped chase away half a million passengers.

One of the starkest comparisons is with the rest of England: the number of people riding on London's buses is the same as on all others operated from Berwick-upon-Tweed to Penzance. That is achieved with 8,500 buses, around one fifth of the number in all of England.

Buses continue to be the most used part of the London transport network. The Underground — also busier than ever — carried 1.23billion passengers in 2012/13.

Elected Mayors

The body that has delivered it is Transport for London, the most recent incarnation of London Transport, which took over from London Regional Transport on 3 July 2000. It is responsible not just for buses and railways, but roads and traffic management, taxis and river buses. As a highway authority, it helps create the priorities needed to speed the flow of buses.

Transport for London was established as a key part of a package of changes to how London is governed, along with an elected Mayor and Greater London Assembly. Its role is to deliver the Mayor's transport strategy, but unlike Greater London Council days its public funding comes from central government,

Transport for London inherited East Thames Buses, formed to take over the services of Harris Bus in February 2000. In 2002 it took over two routes from another failed contractor, London Easylink. One was the cross-river 42 (Liverpool Street-Denmark Hill), operated with 14 unusual 32-seat East Lancs-bodied Scania OmniTowns, which passed to Go-Ahead when it bought East Thames in October 2009. This 2003 view shows ELS6 on Tower Bridge, with the Tower of London and the Gherkin behind. AM

supplementing what it raises from revenue like bus fares, the sale of commercial advertising, surplus property, borrowing and money from third parties for specific projects.

The first elected Mayor was Ken Livingstone, former GLC leader, who stood as an independent candidate in 2000 and back with Labour in 2004. The Conservatives' Boris Johnson defeated him in 2008 and was re-elected in 2012.

Both have stepped enthusiastically into the role of champion and public figurehead for London, arguing with central government for the funding they recognised as being essential for the functioning of one of the world's great capital cities. In their very different ways, they have also built on the consensus in London — in business and politics — that public transport is a vital service that must be funded and expanded to secure much of the money that Transport for London needs.

Heading Transport for London is London's commissioner of transport. Since 2006 that has been Sir Peter Hendy, who joined London Transport as a graduate trainee in 1975, became managing director of the CentreWest bus company in 1989 and led its management/employee buyout five

years later.

One of the UK's biggest bus and train operators, FirstGroup, acquired CentreWest in 1997 and he rose to a senior group role before joining Transport for London at its formation as surface transport managing director, responsible for all non-rail activities. As such, he was instrumental in delivering the huge growth in bus travel and he moved into the top job following the departure of the first commissioner, Bob Kiley, who had come from the New York transport authority.

Part of Transport for London's revenue, and support for expansion of the bus service, comes from a controversial measure in Ken Livingstone's election manifesto in 2000: a congestion charge raised from car and other traffic entering much of the City, West End and some adjoining areas.

He won that election while declaring that he would introduce the measure, something that made it easier to implement and for his successor to accept, although Boris Johnson scrapped a subsequent westward extension of the charging zone.

It was introduced in February 2003 and in anticipation of a move from car to public transport commuting, Transport for London increased the number of

bus services serving the affected area, ensuring — as it has also done for the rest of the 100% tendered bus network — that sufficient buses run to meet peak demand. The peaks form a small part of the day, but if more people wanted to travel then than buses were available, the strategy could have failed.

Although this means that near-empty buses may be around directly after the peaks, the overall increase in passenger numbers is filling up some slack and there are many places — our profile of route 25 on p102 highlights one of them — where buses are busy at most times of day.

Routemaster returns... or does it?

Both Mayors were also elected after making pledges about Routemasters, just as the Labour GLC had been in 1981. Ken Livingstone, with ally Dave Wetzel from GLC days at his side, began to implement this by reacquiring Routemasters from a variety of sources. These buses were heavily refurbished, gaining 21st century engines and gearboxes, and used to add capacity on routes on which the type still operated.

There also was speculation about a new generation of London double-decker with a rear platform, just as had been contemplated around 10 years before.

The Strand in July 2002 and all six westbound buses are Routemasters. The first, second and sixth are Metroline RMLs with shallow blue skirt and radiator grille on route 6. Third is a London United RML with grey waistband on the 9. Second last is a First CentreWest RML with yellow waistband on the 23. Fourth is a Go-Ahead London General refurbished RM on the 11. GB

The move to all red removed such liveries as Metrobus's combination of its former blue and yellow with Transport for London's 80% red. Among the first to wear this, in January 2003, were these lowheight East Lancs-bodied Scania OmniDekkkas. AM

Livingstone also uttered his 'de-humanised moron' quote about anyone who would do anything but keep these icons in perpetual service, but was persuaded otherwise as Transport for London planned for big increases in passenger numbers and 100% wheelchair accessibility.

Bluntly, the Routemaster was too small and cramped, and with a step into its narrow lower saloon gangway also was inaccessible by wheelchair or anyone with serious walking impairments. Although the bus operators could be contracted to operate any type of bus that Transport for London specified, many were concerned about how much longer these 1950s and 1960s machines could keep running.

The challenge was to do this with the minimum of controversy. One of the contracted operators in the 1990s had talked of this having to be a 'series of quiet burials rather than a state funeral', but that was probably wishful thinking. Once it was decided that the Routemasters would go — between August 2003 and December 2005 — much flak was aimed at Transport for London for daring to retire an icon and each quiet burial was anything but, even if the disability lobby welcomed every stage of the move.

The final withdrawal was about as close as a bus will ever get to a state funeral: a slow procession through central and south London amid crowds of spectators.

The controversy was stoked up a deal more by Transport of London's choice of new vehicle for some of its busiest routes: the Mercedes-Benz Citaro bendybus. Not all of these routes used Routemasters, nor did they replace all Routemasters. But because they appeared at the same time as the old buses disappeared, there was an inevitable association.

From the perspective of their supporters, these 415 three-door bendybuses hoovered up huge numbers of people very quickly, they accommodated everyone on one level and were supremely accessible. They were supposed to be capable of holding 150 passengers, one third of them in seats. That was one of the negatives from their opponents' point of view, although that was less of an issue for those who travelled in similar conditions on the tube.

There also was a perception that large numbers of passengers used them without paying a fare (their drivers had no ticket-checking role) and some other road users found them intimidating.

Among the latter was Boris Johnson, a keen cyclist. His 2008 manifesto promised to remove them and that he did. Transport for London organised their replacement by December 2011 with conventional four-wheel buses, mainly double-deckers,

with increased frequencies to maintain passenger capacity.

His promise of a 'new Routemaster' morphed into the New Bus for London double-decker first placed in service in February 2012.

London Transport played a decisive role in bringing low-floor buses to the UK and Transport for London has displayed similar vigour in encouraging the development of low emission technology, notably hybrid electric drive. By 2016, it expects one fifth of the London bus fleet to be hybrids.

The quick fix

Increasing bus service capacity is something that Transport for London recognised from the off was the only rapid way of meeting growing demand for travel.

It also was upgrading the Underground and building the east-west Crossrail line connecting outer suburban commuter trains, as well as creating the orbital London Overground out of separate bits of railway.

But all of that would take time, whereas buses could be introduced almost as quickly as a service was designed, tenders invited to operate it and buses ordered and built.

One of the other major achievements

since 2000 has been to improve the quality as well as the quantity of the bus service. Over the 10 years from 1985, there was a perception that cost saving was the chief goal. That was when secondhand buses of almost any standard were accepted provided they were the right size for the route and when operators persuaded London Transport that a less elaborate specification saved money.

The new regime has delivered consistent reliability, with in excess of 97% of scheduled mileage delivered. A quality incentive scheme rewards tendered service operators for good performance, extending five-year contracts by two years where high standards are achieved.

All this experience — and more — was harnessed when Transport for London played a lead role in organising the efficient operation of public transport during the 2012 London Olympics and Paralympics.

The specification of buses has been raised and tightened, with a range of features — including climate control to improve comfort in hot weather, fire suppression equipment in the engine bays and strict noise limits — to ensure consistency.

Livery variations have also been minimised. Buses are now 100% red with the operator's name and logo displayed within parameters acceptable to Transport for London, and the bulls-eye roundel has returned. While that has taken away what some might regard as the more tasteful colour schemes of the 1990s, it also removed those where supplementary primary colours clashed with red.

The operators have also greatly changed through a succession of takeovers and sales. By 2013, Arriva had added the former London Coaches sightseeing business to its former Leaside, South London and Grey-Green operations, and to the London routes operated by its Kent, Essex and Hertfordshire businesses.

Go-Ahead had added London General, Metrobus, East Thames Buses (a London Buses subsidiary created in 2000 after contractor Harris Bus failed), independents Blue Triangle and Docklands Buses, plus the Northumberland Park and Dagenham operations of First (it acquired them in 1998 with Capital Citybus) to London Central.

Metroline became part of Singapore-based ComfortDelGro in 2000 and acquired London Northern, independents

Armchair and Thorpes, plus much of CentreWest from First. The remainder of First's London business went to Australian-owned Tower Transit.

London United was sold to French transport group Transdev in 1997, having already acquired Westlink. It subsequently acquired London Sovereign (incorporating what had been BTS) and the tendered London bus division of car park operator NCP. In a complex international deal, London United passed from Transdev to RATP, the French state-owned Paris city operator, but Transdev retains London Sovereign. RATP also owns Epsom Coaches Group.

Stagecoach still owns East London and Selkent, having sold them to Australia's Macquarie Bank in 2006 and reacquired them four years later. The other major player is Abellio, part of the Dutch state railway, which owns businesses acquired from National Express Group.

At the time of writing, two smaller businesses also operated tendered bus routes: Sullivan Buses in Potters Bar and CT Plus, a trading wing of Hackney Community Transport.

Cashless travel

The removal of Routemasters was partly made possible by a huge increase in the number of passengers buying tickets off the bus.

That process began with the launch of Travelcard in the 1980s but two measures accelerated it on buses. One was self-service roadside ticket machines in central London, requiring passengers buying single journey tickets (or day bus passes when available) to buy one before riding on a bus.

The other — the bigger and more lasting one — is the Oyster smartcard, introduced in July 2003 and extended greatly in scope since then. Over 43million were issued over the ensuing nine years and by June 2012 it was being used to pay for 80% of all public transport journeys in London. Much of the balance is by rail ticket holders paying for add-on travel and the percentage of passengers paying cash for bus travel is down to a low single figure percentage.

Oyster fares are substantially cheaper than those for cash, which is likely to be used even less following the introduction of contactless debit and credit cards to pay for bus and rail travel.

Such has been the uptake of these new payment methods that Transport for London felt confident it could remove the roadside ticket machines and have drivers collect the few fares from those still paying cash without slowing the service down again.

Another major advance, implemented between 2006 and 2009, was iBus, which combines the automatic location of every bus with audio-visual information on the bus, informing passengers of the route number and final destination as well as the next stop. There also is a wealth of real-time travel information available at bus stops and electronically on passengers' hand-held devices. ■ **AM**

Arriva London MA109, one of 415 Mercedes-Benz Citaro bendybuses operated on Transport for London routes, at Hyde Park Corner. They replaced Routemasters on the 38 on 29 October 2005 and were replaced by a higher frequency of new double-deckers on 14 November 2009. MARK LYONS

A Scania OmniCity and ALX400 TransBus Trident of Stagecoach with a Wright Eclipse Gemini-bodied Volvo B7TL of Arriva in between. JEFF TATTERSALL

TODAY'S
double-deckers

The route tendering system ensures that most buses in London are replaced within a maximum of 14 years, often no more than 12. Five-year contracts, with potential two-year extensions, either specify the use of new or existing vehicles, the existing ones often on condition that they will be refurbished for their second term of use.

When taken out of London service, most either will be sold or — if operated by one of the major bus groups — may be moved on for use by sister companies in other parts of Britain. In either instance, London features like centre doors and powered wheelchair ramps are likely to be removed.

All the current fleet is low-floor and the oldest designs of double-deck body

still in London service are the President and ALX400. The President, produced between 1998 and early 2005, was originally badged as a Plaxton but from around 2002 it became the TransBus President and the last ones built (for Metroline) are badged Alexander Dennis.

Chassis maker Dennis and bodybuilders Plaxton and Alexander merged in 2000 to form TransBus International, which adopted a single brand after about two years. TransBus collapsed in 2004 and new owners renamed it Alexander Dennis. The Wigan factory building the President closed in 2005 and no more were built.

London examples have been built on Dennis or TransBus Trident, Volvo B7TL or DAF DB250 chassis, the Volvo built at a factory in Sweden and the DAF in the Netherlands.

Alexander (later TransBus or Alexander Dennis) built the ALX400 between 1998 and 2005 mainly at its factory in Falkirk, central Scotland but some also were built in the now closed facilities in Belfast and Wigan. It also has been supplied to London on the Trident, B7TL and DAF DB250.

Presidents and ALX400s are operated by Arriva, the former First business, London United and Metroline, while Go-Ahead and CT Plus operate the President only and Abellio and Stagecoach the ALX400. Arriva, Go-Ahead, London United and Metroline all use type codes based on the old London Transport system.

Arriva's Presidents are DLP (DAF), Go-Ahead's are PDN (Trident), PVL and PVN (Volvo), CT Plus's are HTP, London United's are VP, while Metroline's are

TP and TPL (Trident) and VP and VPL (Volvo). Arriva's ALX400s are DLA (DAF) and VLA (Volvo), London United's are TA and TLA (Trident) and VA (Volvo) and Metroline's are TA (Trident).

Alexander Dennis introduced the Enviro400 in 2005. Apart from three on Volvo B9TL chassis for Go-Ahead (type VE), all the London Enviro400s are on the manufacturer's own chassis with Cummins engine. Most are built at Falkirk with chassis from the former Dennis factory in Guildford, but some body and chassis are built at the Plaxton factory in Scarborough.

Type codes are T (Arriva), E (Go-Ahead), ADE (London United) and TE (Metroline). They also are operated by Abellio, the former First business, Epsom Coaches and Stagecoach.

Abellio, Go-Ahead (EH), London United (ADH), Metroline (TEH) and Stagecoach have the hybrid version, Enviro400H.

The Wright Eclipse Gemini was been built in Northern Ireland from 2001 on the Volvo B7TL for Arriva (VLW), First, Go-Ahead (WVL, VWL) and the similar Pulsar Gemini on the DAF (later VDL) DB250 for Arriva (DW). Abellio also has Eclipse Geminis.

The Eclipse Gemini 2, on Volvo B9TL has been built since 2009 for First, Go-Ahead (WVL, WVN) and Metroline (VW) and the Cummins-powered Gemini 2DL (with VDL-built chassis parts) went to First but mainly Arriva (DW). The Gemini 2 is also built on Volvo B5LH hybrid chassis for Arriva (HV), Go-Ahead (WHV) and Metroline (VWH).

Scania double-deckers operated in London are the OmniDekka bodied by

A TransBus President-bodied Trident of Metroline. PHIL HALEWOOD

An Arriva Enviro400. STEVE MASKELL

East Lancs (mainly with Metrobus) and the OmniCity built at Scania's factory in Poland and operated by CT Plus (SD), the part of First transferring to Metroline, Metrobus, London United (SP) and Stagecoach (bought while its London business was owned by Macquarie Bank).

East Lancs and successor company Optare built a newer double-deck body, the Olympus, on Scania and other chassis. The largest concentration is on 54 Alexander Dennis Enviro400 chassis at Go-Ahead (type DOE).

Experimental types include two Volvo B9TLs with Egyptian-built MCV bodies (both numbered VM1) with Go-Ahead and London United. ∎

Go-Ahead London WVL482, a Wright Eclipse Gemini 2-bodied Volvo B9TL. STEVE MASKELL

An Enviro200 in First's London fleet. This is the part of the business sold to Metroline. RICHARD GODFREY

TODAY'S single-deckers

By far the most common single-deck types in London today are the Dennis (later TransBus or Alexander Dennis) Dart and its successor introduced from 2006, the Enviro200. There was an overlap between the end of one and the start of the other.

This has a Cummins engine and Allison automatic gearbox. Most Darts have the Pointer body built by Plaxton at Scarborough until 2001 and at Falkirk after that. They continued to be badged as Plaxton products into 2003, before TransBus applied its brand universally. They latterly were Alexander Dennis products.

Until 2001, Alexander built its ALX200 body on the Dart. Arriva, Metroline and Stagecoach were among its London customers.

Arriva, which has a long established import arrangement with the Dutch manufacturer, persuaded DAF Bus

(now VDL Bus) to develop a Cummins-powered low-floor single-decker similar to the Dart, which for London has a Wright Cadet body and fleetnumber class DWL and DWS.

Type codes for Darts include PDL (Arriva), LDP (Go-Ahead) and DPS (London United and Transdev London). For Enviro200s they include EN and ENL (Arriva), SE and SEN (Go-Ahead), DE (London United and Transdev), plus DE and DEM (Metroline). London United has five Enviro200H hybrids (HDE).

Metroline and Go-Ahead have Egyptian-built MCV bodies on either Dart, Enviro200 or German-built MAN chassis, while Metrobus has some Enviro200 bodies on MAN chassis and Go-Ahead has Optare Esteem bodies on Enviro200 chassis (type SOE).

The other similar-sized single-deckers include the Wright StreetLite introduced from 2010 and built in two

versions, Door Forward (wheels behind the front door) and Wheel Forward (front and only door behind the front wheels). Go-Ahead (type WS) operates both versions.

There also are some Optare Versas with London United (OV) and Stagecoach. CT Plus and Epsom Coaches are among London operators of the smaller Optare Solo, some with two doors.

Long single-deckers remain in a minority, used mainly on the former Red Arrow central London routes and a few others that require bigger buses but have physical restrictions like low bridges. Most are the Mercedes-Benz Citaro operated by Go-Ahead (MEC), London United and Epsom Coaches (MCL) and Stagecoach.

Metrobus operates the single-deck Scania OmniCity, while London United has some Mercedes-powered Optare Tempos (type OT).

WS18, a Door Forward Wright StreetLite new to Go-Ahead in 2013. RICHARD GODFREY

Optare Esteem-bodied Enviro200 SOE8 of Go-Ahead London General. MARK LYONS

The Heritage Routemasters

Perfectly preserved traditional double-deckers operate a regular service every day connecting some of the picture postcard attractions of central London

Even before the last 'real' Routemaster ran in London service in December 2005, Transport for London recognised the great affection for — and tourist potential of — these iconic buses.

Although the move to 100% low-floor accessible buses sounded the Routemaster's final death-knell, there was an appetite to give Londoners, visitors and enthusiasts the opportunity to hop on and off an open platform bus.

So as many were mourning the imminent end of normal Routemaster operation, TfL hatched a cunning plan. Where, it mused, would the tourists want to go on these weird British buses? Not perhaps Paddington Basin-Streatham, the journey of the 159, the last Routemaster service; not Victoria-Stoke Newington (the 73, another late

Routemaster survivor). Although the 11 (St Paul's, Trafalgar Square, Whitehall, Parliament Square) might have seemed to be the obvious choice, TfL settled for the 9 and 15.

The 9, operated then by First (and about to pass to Tower Transit), runs between Aldwych and Hammersmith. End to end it may not seem a contender, but between Albert Hall and Aldwych TfL decided it was ideal for Routemasters. That covered the Strand, Trafalgar Square, Piccadilly, Hyde Park Corner, Kensington, Knightsbridge and the Royal Albert Hall. Today it runs between Trafalgar Square and High Street Kensington.

And the 15, operated then and now by Stagecoach, seemed a likely candidate. End to end it operates between Blackwall Station and Regent Street but the Routemasters just cover the section

between Tower Hill and Trafalgar Square, taking in the Tower of London, Eastcheap, Cannon Street, St Paul's Cathedral, Ludgate Hill, Fleet Street, the Royal Courts of Justice and the Strand.

The 16 refurbished buses allocated to the heritage Routemaster routes (five for each route, plus six spares) are probably in the eyes of the purist not real Routemasters — but to the average passenger they are. They are 64-seat double-deckers with a driver in a cab at the front and a conductor on the open rear platform.

The Heritage 9 and 15 appear to run every 20min daily between 10.00 and 18.00 (although the TfL website suggests the 15 runs every 15 minutes).

These services started in November 2005, just weeks before the last day of Routemasters on the 159, and although they have never been promoted very hard they are very visible and have an obvious appeal to tourists, while many locals enjoy still being able to hop on and off. And with their Cummins engines and modern gearboxes, they are more environmentally acceptable than the

Left: RM2089 passing St Paul's. Several of these refurbished buses were bought back from other owners in 2000 when Transport for London needed more Routemasters. This one came from Reading Mainline.

original AECs or Leylands, even if they don't sound quite the same.

A trip on the heritage Routemasters is, depending on your interest, a good way to see some London sights, or a chance to relive memories of open platform buses. Or perhaps a bit of both. As both routes terminate at Trafalgar Square, one from the east, the other from the west, it seemed sensible on a recent visit to London to start at one outer terminus and work my way to the other.

Starting at Tower Hill at midday with Stagecoach's route 15 on the Sunday of a 2013 bank holiday weekend, the area is buzzing with tourists, with open-top buses from various operators picking up and setting down, while those opting for the cheaper alternative (£2.40 cash fare, £1.40 with an Oyster card) wait for the 15.

As there is little publicity for the Heritage services at stops, the waiting crowd may well have seen a previous departure and waited 20min for the next. All that the bus stop timetables state is that 'Heritage Routemasters operate additional journeys', declaring the times and noting that 'These journeys cannot carry wheelchairs'.

What's not to like? Purists may complain about the modern engine and the 'wrong' seat moquette and interior colours, but to these people they simply say 'old bus' that you can enjoy boarding at the rear and paying fares to a roving conductor. To visitors they are as much 'London' as black cabs and red phone boxes.

Tower Hill presents a mix of vistas, from the centuries-old Tower to the Shard, the Gherkin and other new blocks that are changing the London skyline. And a reminder of the ever-evolving technology of modern buses, a hydrogen fuel-cell bus on the RV1 route.

My 15 heads through a fairly deserted City, through the canyons of Cannon Street into the open spaces around St

The Routemasters offer a striking contrast when running alongside modern low-floor double-deckers. RM1218 and an Enviro400H hybrid pause for pedestrians at Trafalgar Square.

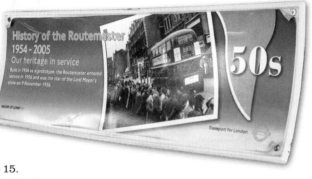

Posters inside tell the Routemaster story. This one shows prototype RM1 in the 1956 Lord Mayor's Show parade.

Paul's. Some passengers waiting for a 15 are surprised when a 49-year old Routemaster hoves into view rather than the 61-plate hybrids that are the normal offering. Some instinctively make for the front of the bus to board but the conductor calls them to the rear, and while a few seem puzzled by this anachronistic apparition, most seem delighted. Passers-by smile and point when they see our Routemaster and capture it on their camera phones.

Through a deserted Fleet Street and past the Royal Courts of Justice, RM2050 dawdles; it's a very different matter on weekdays when the volume of traffic can cause timing problems. Into The Strand on the last leg of the journey and passengers are dropped outside Charing Cross station. The end-to-end journey time is 24min.

Compared to the square mile of the City, Trafalgar Square is teeming with visitors and to catch a westbound 9, passengers must negotiate this busy junction to a stop in Cockspur Street where the 9 picks up.

My steed this time is RM1218, which saunters past St James's Palace – though not before a tour guide with a phalanx of followers has imperiously held up the traffic to allow her large party to crocodile across the road. Into Piccadilly and traffic is heavier, and we pass LT4, a New Bus for London, heading to Hackney Central on the 38 – two London-designed buses separated by nearly 50 years.

The driver expertly negotiates the multi-lane racetrack that is Hyde Park Corner into Knightsbridge and the heavy Sunday afternoon traffic. RM1218 threads its way past Hyde Park and some ultra-expensive homes to Kensington High Street, where the route suddenly ends at Warwick Gardens, perhaps not the most obvious tourist destination, but a good place to turn. The scheduled end-to-end timing is 30min, and we took 32, despite heavy traffic.

The Routemasters look curiously small, rounded and slightly vulnerable among today's low-floor double-deckers, and, yes, they seem cramped and noisy, but it is to be hoped that TfL sees fit to keep this little enterprise going as an acknowledgement of the years of service the Routemaster has given to London — currently 54 and counting. ■ **GB**

Hybrids & electrics

In a quest for lower exhaust emissions and better air quality, London is on course for having a fifth of its buses powered as hybrid electrics by 2016

Just as London Transport took the lead in bringing low-floor accessible buses to Britain, so also has Transport for London been a prime mover in the development of hybrid electric and other ultra-low or zero emissions buses.

Part of the reason for this is that air quality targets have been set for cities across Europe and to meet these — and avoid financial penalties — London has to reduce the harmful emissions in its atmosphere. Transport is one of the major sources of these emissions and Transport for London needs to reduce those coming from the 8,500 buses operated on its routes.

European legislation has played a part in cutting these, with progressively tougher limits imposed on the content of the exhaust from all diesel engines in new buses, coaches and lorries from 1992. These standards had progressed from Euro1 to Euro5 by 2008, with Euro6 due to be mandatory from 2014, making modern engines far cleaner than their predecessors.

These rules apply only to new vehicles built after the various starting dates for each new standard and in February 2008

One of the original Wright Electrocity hybrids for Go-Ahead, WHY2, in Bessborough Street, Pimlico following conversion to the Cummins/Siemens driveline. MARK LYONS

Transport for London created a low-emission zone (LEZ) covering much of the area within the M25 and affecting all buses, coaches, lorries, minibuses, vans, motor caravans and taxis. These initially required all vehicles — other than pre-1973 historic ones — to meet some Euro3 standards, this being increased to some Euro4 standards starting in 2012.

Older standard engines may still be used provided the exhaust system is

adapted to clean up their emissions, but by 2016 the current aim is that all Transport for London buses will be at least of Euro4 standard mandatory on new vehicles since October 2005. Exhaust after-treatment is being fitted in older buses to meet these new limits.

All this has been happening against a background of buses becoming heavier. The 64-seat Routemaster weighed 7.25tonne unladen, while a modern

Left: **First operated its five Ford-powered Wright Gemini 2HEV hybrids on route 328 between Golders Green and Chelsea Worlds End, where WNH39002 was waiting between journeys in April 2009, with a Wright-bodied Volvo B7TL diesel parked behind. The first hybrids all advertised their credentials with green leaves and a prominent explanation of how they were powered.** AM

double-decker with no more seats is easily 5tonnes heavier. Yes, it is around 3m — one third — longer, but its seats are a lot heavier, the climate control, wheelchair accessibility, fire prevention and exhaust cleaning extras all pile on the kilogrammes.

More weight means more fuel is consumed and ironically the measures adopted by engine manufacturers to meet the emissions standards up to and including Euro3 also increased fuel consumption. The smoke coming out of the tailpipe may have been a lot cleaner than before, but more fuel was being burnt to achieve that.

This led Transport for London and many others to recognise that something else was needed if there were to be meaningfully large reductions in exhaust emissions from buses. That implied some kind of electrification.

Cumulo bus

Back in the 1980s, London Transport had participated in a trial of an early attempt at this when it operated a development vehicle from Volvo. This was Alexander-bodied Volvo Citybus C1, an underfloor-engined double-decker in which the normal gearbox was replaced by something called a Flygmotor Cumulo. This collected kinetic energy when the brakes were applied and released it to reduce the load on the engine as it accelerated again.

C1 arrived in London in 1985 and operated between July 1986 and September 1987 on inter-suburban route 102 in north London.

Over the ensuing 20 years the idea developed of hybrid technology, propelling buses by a combination of electric drive and conventional diesel. Two forms of this propulsion exist: parallel or series drive.

With parallel drive, the engine drives the wheels as in a conventional diesel bus, but batteries — topped up by energy recovered when braking — power the electric motor, which pulls the bus away from stops before the diesel cuts in again. This reduces the biggest strain on the diesel engine and with it the times when the biggest amounts of fuel would be consumed.

With series drive, instead of driving the wheels, the diesel engine powers the

generator that charges the batteries, which in turn power the electric motor that drives the wheels.

The United States military has been operating hybrid vehicles for nearly 30 years and the technology began to be applied to some urban buses there, with New York being particularly enthusiastic for a time in replacing some of its diesel buses with hybrids.

Two of the leading manufacturers of buses for London — Wrightbus and TransBus (now Alexander Dennis) — began developing hybrid buses at the start of the 21st century, with single-deck prototypes unveiled by Wrightbus in 2002 and TransBus in 2003. Transport for London soon announced plans for a trial of 12 of them — expected to be six of each type — on Go-Ahead London-operated route 360, which links Royal Albert Hall and Elephant & Castle by skirting around the edge of innermost central London.

The trial was delayed until February 2006 when six Wright Electrocity single-deckers went into service. In the four years since the first Electrocity had been revealed, Wrightbus had changed the technology. It originally had an American-built micro turbine in place of a normal engine, but had moved on to use a small diesel from a Vauxhall Astra car.

The Electrocity was based on a VDL SB120 chassis supplied to Wrightbus

The Optare Versa hybrid demonstrator built for trials in London. Stagecoach and London United have diesel Versas. AM

Rear view of a Wright Eclipse Gemini 2-bodied Volvo B5LH of Arriva. The engine is in the rear left-hand corner. AM

without engine or gearbox and fitted with what on a diesel bus would be a Wright Cadet body.

TransBus had collapsed in 2004 and although Alexander Dennis continued the work it had done with its Enviro200H hybrid prototypes, it also made some changes in technology before eventually adopting the American-built HybriDrive system from BAE Systems, technology already used in New York and elsewhere in North America.

There were inevitable teething problems with the new buses and Transport for London had to revise its ambitions for hybrids — at one point it hoped to be specifying only hybrids for new buses from 2012 — as manufacturers and operators went through the pain barrier of turning a largely untried idea into practical technology.

Hybrids also were around 50% more expensive than diesels. The expectation was that they would use between 25% and 30% less fuel, but the difference in purchase price needed to be funded. The longer-term hope was that if they became commonplace, manufacturers would reduce the price of their hybrids.

Double-deckers arrive

Single-deckers may have been fine for the initial trial, but what London really wanted were hybrid double-deckers and Wrightbus obliged in October 2006 with its prototype Gemini HEV (for Hybrid Electric Vehicle) using similar technology to the single-deckers. It went into service the following February with Arriva on route 141 between London Bridge and Palmers Green, part of which replaced trolleybus route 641 in November 1961, on extended loan from the manufacturer.

By 2009, there were 56 hybrids in six London fleets. Go-Ahead had five — the six original Electrocitys plus a seventh to improved specification, a Gemini HEV double-decker and five Alexander Dennis Enviro400H double-deckers. Next biggest collection was 11 at Arriva — five

One of the Wright Pulsar-bodied VDL hydrogen fuel-cell buses at London Bridge. The roof is raised to accommodate hydrogen cylinders. RICHARD GODFREY

Gemini 2HEV and six Wright-bodied Volvo B5LH double-deckers.

Metroline had 10 — five Enviro400Hs and five Optare Tempo single-deckers, London United the only five Enviro200Hs for London and two Enviro400Hs. First had five Gemini 2HEVs and East London (then owned by Macquarie Bank) had five Tempos.

The Volvos and Optares had parallel drive systems, the others series drive. Volvo makes its own hybrid drive, while Optare used an Allison system from America. The Wrightbus system was by Siemens, but it had moved from Vauxhall to Ford engines on the double-deckers before concluding that the larger four-cylinder Cummins engine used by Alexander Dennis was better suited to buses.

The 10 Optare vehicles are the only ones of their kind, the Yorkshire-based manufacturer having since moved to Siemens series drive. It built a hybrid version of a Versa single-decker with hybrid drive for trials in London, but the sums for hybrid buses add up best with double-deckers — extra cost of the drive system less the amount of fuel saved — and only six other hybrid single-deckers have been built for London operators since 2009.

These are the Electrocitys needed to complete the conversion of route 360. They arrived in 2011 and have Cummins engines and new generation batteries; the original six have been rebuilt to the same standard. The five Abellio Electrocitys have all been taken out of service and the Tempos see somewhat limited use.

Aiming for 20%

The Go-Ahead Gemini HEV has returned to Wrightbus, which at the time of writing was in the process of rebuilding the 10 Gemini 2HEVs of Arriva and First to a driveline similar to New Bus for London, with Cummins engine in place of the less durable Ford van engines, although First's five were expected to move out of London.

Thanks in part to several rounds of the government's Green Bus Fund, paying some of the difference in price between hybrid and conventional diesel buses, the London hybrid fleet has grown substantially and although standard diesels are still being built for London is expected to exceed 1,700 double-deckers — 20% of the total — by 2016. That will

An Alexander Dennis Enviro400H of Abellio with the more restrained 'hybrid' branding in green ahead of the rear wheel. MARK LYONS

include the 608 New Bus for London double-deckers from Wrightbus.

Not only does London have the largest number of hybrid buses anywhere in Britain, but it also has the largest number anywhere in Europe.

Besides the surviving earlier vehicles, there are Enviro400Hs with Abellio, CT Plus, the former First business, Go-Ahead, London United, Metroline and Stagecoach, while Arriva, Go-Ahead and Metroline operate Wright-bodied Volvos, with 23 more due in autumn 2013 for Transdev London Sovereign to replace Scania OmniDekka diesels on former Routemaster route 13.

Hybrids have been targeted on routes passing through known low air quality hotspots in a drive to reduce pollution and diminish the risk of incurring fines from Europe.

Fuel-cells and batteries

Transport for London's drive for emissions reductions has not ended with hybrids. Indeed it began before the first hybrids arrived when, between September 2004 and January 2007, First operated three Mercedes-Benz Citaro single-deckers with hydrogen fuel-cells as part of an international trial of this type of vehicle. They ran on route 25 and later on the RV1 tourist route connecting Covent Garden and Tower Gateway, next to Tower Bridge and the Tower of London.

This technology uses hydrogen as a fuel to power a miniature on-board power station that generates the

electricity needed to propel them quietly and with a light plume of steam and droplets of water their only emissions.

Following the trial, the fuel-cell equipment was removed and the buses were donated to museums, one of them to the London Transport Museum's Acton Depot annex. Mercedes-Benz used some of the lessons learned in this trial for the development of a second generation of fuel-cell Citaro, but none of these has so far been built for London.

However, Transport for London has acquired its own second-generation fuel-cell fleet for continued trials on the RV1. These are eight 11.9m Wright-bodied VDL SB200s with American-built Ballard fuel-cells. Five arrived in 2010/11, the other three — delayed by the collapse of a component supplier in America — in 2013. Operation of these buses transferred to Tower Transit on the sale of First's London business.

Fuel-cell technology is still extremely expensive and in order to test more conventional battery electric drive, six 12m single-deckers are to operate alongside 12m diesel Citaros on the former Red Arrow routes, which may lend themselves to off-peak battery charging because of the need for some buses to run only at peak periods.

These vehicles, packed with batteries on the roof and over the front wheels, are coming from Chinese manufacturer BYD (the initials are for Build Your Dreams), which is establishing a European factory in Romania. ■ **AM**

New Bus for London

New Bus for London, delivered at the end of 2011 and first into service in February 2012, is the first purpose-designed double-decker for London since Routemaster production ended in 1968.

It is built by Wrightbus in Northern Ireland and designed by that company in close co-operation with Transport for London and Thomas Heatherwick Studios, the internationally acclaimed design studio also responsible for the 2012 Olympic flame.

It is a diesel-electric hybrid with 62 seats, two staircases (front and rear) and three doors (front, centre and rear). The rear door can be left open when an attendant is on duty, allowing passengers to hop on and off between stops when the bus is stationary and the attendant judges it safe to do so. In this mode, passengers may board and alight at stops through all three doors, as was the case with bendybuses.

In the quiet hours of the evening and night when there is no attendant, it works more like other one-person-operated buses: passengers board by the front and exit by the other two.

By 2016 there should be 608 of them, all owned by Transport for London and leased to operators as part of their contract to operate particular routes. That is eight prototypes and 600 production versions. The prototypes were supplied to Arriva to operate alongside Wright Gemini 2DLs on route 38. The first batches of production buses are allocated to Metroline for the 24 and Go-Ahead for the 11. All are expected to operate on the busiest London routes.

Joint winner of the design competition was this concept from Aston Martin and Foster+Partners. The shape may have influenced the execution of the LT.
TRANSPORT FOR LONDON

New Bus for London prototype LT2 operating through Islington on route 38. These eight were supplied with special LT61 and LT12 registrations with letters from AHT to HHT.
STEPHEN WHITELEY

Regardless of who operates them, they are classed in a single numbering series from LT1 to LT608 with their own series of Belfast registration numbers from LTZ 1001 upwards.

The LT classification acknowledges the earlier holder of that moniker, the six-wheel AEC Renown of 1929, which was regarded as a revolutionary vehicle in its time, just as New Bus for London is in the second decade of the 21st century. The sweep of windows around its rear staircase also are in the shape of the open stair of an early original LT.

It has no other name. Wrightbus has names for all of its bus products. Many of these used to be quite military, like Commander, Crusader and Cadet, or

have a cosmic connection like Solar, Eclipse and Pulsar. More recently it has given them Street-prefixed names. Given the freedom to name New Bus for London, StreetMaster might have been appropriate, but it does not have the freedom. The rights to this design belong to Transport for London.

Mayor Boris Johnson apparently was not persuaded by suggestions that it should have a name, unofficially instead of its four-word official name or type letters it is referred to either as a New Routemaster, the Boris Bus or Borismaster. Popular culture has also given us Boris Bikes — cycles to rent from Transport for London — and Boris Island, the Thames Estuary airport the Mayor has been campaigning for as a replacement for Heathrow.

Routemaster competition

The bus community prefers Borismaster and there is good reason to link Mayor and bus: it might not have been created

without him and certainly would not have a hop-on/hop-off facility had that not been one of his bigger electoral pledges in 2008.

Back then, his goal was simple: to develop a new Routemaster, an open rear platform double-decker fit for the exhaust emissions and accessibility requirements of today, two of the factors that had helped sweep the 1950s Routemaster off the network by the end of 2005. It would be his contribution to the London bus story in the way that Ken Livingstone's had been perceived to be the bendybus.

So everyone from serious automotive designers to the general public, adults and children, were invited to enter a competition with a prize pot of £85,000 for the various winners.

This attracted around 700 entries and by December 2008 the results were announced. Two winners shared the £50,000 first prize for designs — a partnership of sports car manufacturer

Aston Martin and the Foster+Partners architecture practice, and bus design engineering consultancy Capoco, which among other things was behind the hugely successful Dennis Dart and Optare Solo.

All the entries were very much in the shape of the Routemaster, with wheels under the driver and a door at the back, as well as wheelchair access towards the front. The Aston Martin/ Foster vehicle had a curved shape of its own, while Capoco's looked a lot more like a Routemaster and like many of the entries had a vertically divided grille complete with space for an AEC triangle.

The downright frivolous — but fun — ideas included a Routemaster reconfigured as some kind of mobile Jacuzzi.

Because of the design brief, what they all proposed was a bigger, updated take on an old — if for a long time successful — way of configuring a London double-decker.

Competition design ideas included this six-wheel modern Routemaster by Alexander Crolla. TRANSPORT FOR LONDON

Groundbreaking project

It was what happened next that turned what might have been a piece of retro indulgence into a potentially groundbreaking urban bus.

Transport for London took the ideas along with its own thoughts on how bus design might move forward and at the same time sought bids from manufacturers prepared to work with it to build prototypes and hopefully put it into production. Those thoughts fairly quickly settled on three doors and two staircases and a design capable of operating for part of the day without an attendant.

Six were shortlisted but as discussions progressed and both the design brief and timescale became clear, it soon fell to three. As two of Europe's leading mass producers of largely single-deck buses, Mercedes-Benz and Scania soon concluded that this was not for them. Too few buses and too early a delivery date. Tata Hispano, an Indian-owned Spanish bus builder also was in the early shortlist.

Transport for London's immovable requirement was to go from concept to operational prototypes within four years — the Mayor's first term of office. It had taken nine years with the Routemaster.

That left the three UK bus builders. One of them, Optare — which had been talking of building a low-floor double-decker since at least 2000 and for a time had ideas of a side-engined layout as on London Transport's stillborn XRM — dropped out.

Wrightbus, which had researched the exercise in part by taking an old Routemaster apart, was selected over Alexander Dennis, which had offered two designs in co-operation with Capoco. Transport for London brought

LT1 on test in Oxford Street in February 2012, shortly before the first of these buses went into service. One of the senior project leaders, David Hampson-Ghani, is standing next to the driver. MARK PITMAN

LT2 leaving Victoria on the 38, behind a Metroline Enviro400H hybrid on the 16. The attendant can be seen holding on to the vertical stanchion on the open rear platform. MARK LYONS

Heatherwick Studios in to provide styling and design expertise from the fresh perspective of people with no prior knowledge of buses.

Heatherwick challenged Wrightbus to go beyond the natural conservatism of a bus builder, while Wrightbus put a cautionary brake on Heatherwick when it knew the designers' more ambitious ideas — like glazing stretching down to kerb level — would be impractical on a vehicle likely to hit or be hit at slow speed in busy streets and garages.

Results of that partnership included solid front panels disguised as glass and, on the rear staircase, small pieces of glass bonded next to each other to give the impression of one large single window. The rounded shape of the bus also eliminates sharp corners often vulnerable to accident damage.

Interior design

One of the most impressive things about the new LT has been that it has preserved its appearance from

The Routemaster-influenced interior looking towards the rear downstairs.

View towards the back of the top deck.

An LT beginning to take shape at Wrightbus.

the unveiling of the first artist's impressions through the building of a full-size mock-up to prototypes and production.

It has been designed to make a feature of its most prominent parts, like the wrap-round rising glazed area around the rear staircase and an S-shaped window arrangement for the front stairs.

Like the Aston Martin/Foster design winner, all its corners are rounded. By comparison with other recent double-deckers in London, the upper deck windows are quite shallow — deliberately so, as less glass also means less weight. It also makes the bus less likely to become uncomfortably hot in

summer, behaving less like a mobile greenhouse.

It relies entirely on mechanical ventilation, having no opening windows although the option of fitting them is built into the design. This is incorporated into the ceilings, which are more curved as a result, but that avoids having the more intrusive units fitted in the tops of staircases of many other London double-deckers.

Something that impresses many first-time riders is the interior finish. Here, Transport for London has raised standards way beyond the sometimes barely cushioned and clinically coloured appearance of other vehicles. The seats are the closest in a generation to the deep pile comfort of the likes of a Routemaster or RT.

They also are upholstered in a modern design that takes its colour cues from the original Routemaster. So too does the interior panelling, in a combination of burgundy and cream. And Routemaster-style Treadmaster flooring, sourced from a supplier of decking for yachts, completes the effect.

Chassis design

New Bus for London has been designed from the outset as a hybrid electric. There is no straight diesel equivalent. Its four-cylinder Cummins engine sits under the rear staircase, generating power as needed to charge the batteries that power an electric motor ahead of the rear wheels. German multinational manufacturer Siemens supplies the electric drive system.

For part of the time, like other series hybrid buses, it rides quietly in electric mode only, the engine cutting in as required.

The chassis, built at a separate factory in Antrim about 10 miles from the

Wrightbus body plant in Ballymena, also has independent front suspension to ride out the worst road bumps and potholes and the steering has an impressively tight turning circle, even though at 11.3m (37ft) it is longer than most other London double-deckers.

Those who have driven it say it performs as smoothly as a trolleybus and that the rounded corners enhance drivers' visibility.

The prototypes on route 38 have been returning appreciably better fuel consumption than other hybrids, which in turn produce much better fuel economy than straight diesels. At 12,460kg, the first production vehicles are nearly 200kg lighter than the prototypes, suggesting that together with other refinements there should be a further improvement in fuel economy.

The New Bus for London design includes a future two-door variant that would omit the centre door. It is possible that such a layout could also appear on other double-deckers should manufacturers choose to produce them and that the New Bus for London design could have a life beyond the 608 buses already running or on their way, possibly even a life beyond London.

One thing that Transport for London has made clear is that having invested around £11 million in developing the design and eight prototypes and up to £350,000 on each production bus (the latter not wildly different from the price of other hybrids), it will keep them operating in London for the full 14 years.

Given what happened with Routemasters, RTs and RFs — the previous bespoke buses for London — and allowing for technological changes, they might even have a London life beyond that. ■ **AM**

Route 38

The 38 has many claims to fame. It was one of the last routes to be operated by Routemasters, which survived right up to 2005, then one of the busiest to be converted to articulated buses. Following conversion back to double-deckers in 2009, it became the London route with the largest number of buses (68, by some counts). That's almost as many buses as make up an entire fleet in a town the size of, say, Ipswich.

The 38 is now also celebrated as the first route to see daily operation by the LT-class New Bus for London. The eight prototypes were allocated to the route early in 2012, and six remained in service as we prepare this article, the others having gone off on a prestigious world tour. Although Arriva, a subsidiary of the German state-owned Deutsche Bahn group, runs the route, the LTs are leased from Transport for London.

They run alongside a normal allocation made up mostly of Wright Gemini 2DL integral double-deckers, which combine the familiar Gemini body shape with VDL (formerly DAF) chassis modules

and Cummins engines. Strange to think Wrightbus also builds the LTs; they could hardly look more different. A few Alexander Dennis Enviro400s also appear on the route from time to time, adding further interest to the mix.

At its southern end the 38 starts from Victoria station, then wends its way diagonally through the West End and out to Hackney, in north-east London. It's such a busy route that it has a stand at Victoria bus station to itself (shared only

A northbound 38 at Sadlers Wells Theatre on Rosebery Avenue. This is one of Arriva's Gemini 2DL integrals.

Left: **A New Bus for London prototype in Piccadilly Circus en route for Victoria.**

Right: **A mass of signs as a 38 heads north through Hackney Central.**

with the N38, the night bus equivalent), and this is seldom without a line of buses ready for the next journey.

We set off north up Grosvenor Place, past the high wall hiding Buckingham Palace Gardens on the right, then negotiate the thronging traffic navigating its way around the Hyde Park Corner roundabout. Then we turn north-east into Piccadilly. Passing the Royal Academy, Fortnum & Mason and the Ritz, we reach Piccadilly Circus and head on past the theatres of Shaftesbury Avenue.

To take account of a one-way system, the northbound route makes a long detour at Cambridge Circus, turning north up Charing Cross Road, then rejoining the southbound route in New Oxford Street. Then we quickly fork left along Bloomsbury Way and Theobalds Road.

Not so many pedestrians as we head up Rosebery Avenue, an indeterminate hinterland of offices and upmarket apartments. The modern frontage of Sadlers Wells Theatre looms on the left, a lone straggler from the theatreland we've just left behind.

Then it's back into bustle in busy, trendy Islington, where the raised footpath along Upper Street gives the place the air of a market town. Shopping, smart restaurants, and glimpsed to the side, the curving frontage of the Business Design Centre and The Screen on the Green cinema.

As we head up Essex Road, the effect of Islington Borough's recently-imposed 20mph speed limit becomes apparent. Presumably this reduces accidents, but it feels as if we're crawling along in heavy traffic even when we're not.

After pausing to photograph some of the 38s on their journey, we spot an LT approaching and try our luck at boarding it between stops. Luckily it pauses at the traffic lights at New North Road, so we cross warily and trot up to it. Raising an eyebrow tentatively to the conductor, we're greeting by a beckoning smile. 'Yes, come aboard!'

The maroon and grey interior is refined; it's reminiscent of Routemasters in their heyday. And the ride is extraordinary: extremely smooth and vibration-free, and when the diesel engine periodically cuts out and it runs on batteries only, almost silent.

At Balls Pond Road we turn east, crossing the busy north-south Kingsland Road at Dalston, then onward along Graham Road. Distinctive three- and four-storey Victorian flats and town houses line much of this part of our route.

Hackney feels like a substantial township with its own identity. Particularly surprising is the one-way section of the main through route, Mare Street — the part that runs north of the railway bridge. Here it narrows to a meandering lane, forming the hub of the shopping area, and vaguely evoking the older parts of Brighton or York.

Half the buses on the 38 terminate at Hackney Garage, just under the bridge, but the rest head on north into lower Clapton, another sprawl of Victorian shops. The terminus is still called Clapton Pond, and there really is a pond, set in a small garden that has recently been refurbished, and now looks very smart.

However, unlike the Routemasters that used to line up under a terrace of houses by the pond, the 38s now continue a few hundred metres north to the new Lea Bridge roundabout, where a bus stand partly shrouded by trees has been created in the middle. Truly a case of ever-diminishing circles. ■ **PR**

Above: **The Screen on the Green in Islington.**

Below: **The Clapton Pond turning circle.**

Centenary visions

With bus technology moving internationally towards urban electrification, could London embrace some of the features of the trolleybuses that ran until just over 50 years ago?

SG1 trolleybus and Pushley Mk3 taxi.

What will London's buses be like in 2033 when Transport for London marks London Transport's centenary? As with all forecasting — like London Transport's over-optimistic postwar predictions of how many buses it would need by 1960 — we can only look at what has happened and is happening and try and guess where technology and travel trends might lead.

Something entirely new and unexpected may be waiting around the corner to take us all by surprise.

The Mayor and Transport for London are building their plans on the assumption that the population will be approaching 10million by 2030, with a need for a million more homes and better transport links. Besides extensions to the Underground, Croydon Tramlink and construction of a north/south Crossrail line, the plans also envisage there being 2,000 New Bus for London double-deckers on the road by 2020.

Those are the official plans, but Alan Page from Rochester has offered us his own ideas of a London beyond 2020 with electric vehicles based more on the trolleybuses that served parts of the UK capital from 1931 until 1962, with a bit of imagination about how this might all happen and just how quickly the technology could advance.

Certainly, cities in Europe and Asia are looking at new ways of making their buses run on electricity, with fast charging points at bus stops and termini.

With hybrids, fuel-cells and battery electrics, Transport for London is moving in that direction. It may feel that the public would not accept the sight of overhead trolleybus wires suspended once again between buildings, but here are Mr Page's ideas to enjoy.

Sunbeams with solar panels

His first vehicle on route 76 is what he calls a Sunbeam MF3, a three-axle product of the New Sunbeam Electric Vehicle Company of Wolverhampton. It looks like the MCV-bodied Volvo B9TL diesels in trial service with two of today's London operators.

'It enjoys many of the benefits of current vehicle technology,' he tells us, 'but more importantly it has lightweight, light-reactive solar panels on the roof, allowing the bus to produce as much electricity as it consumes throughout the year.'

The little yellow tricycles are Pushley taxis, capable of carrying two passengers plus luggage. They have a 15mph top speed and the front wheel has a low friction alternator that engages when the driver reaches 5mph.

The buses in his Oxford Street picture are what he calls the Electric Boris, a shortened two-door trolleybus version of the New Bus for London. The Pushley taxis in this picture have a gyro motor that also has been adopted for the

The MCV-like Sunbeam MF3. Pictures by ALAN PAGE

Electric Boris, enabling this design to produce twice as much electricity as it consumes.

Such has been the success of these developments that Sunbeam has gone on to produce the SG1 trolleybus for widespread throughout the UK, as operated on route 780. This produces three times the power that it consumes, thanks to the addition of chilled bearings on the gyro motors and liquid compression gearing. The four-wheel Pushley Mk3 taxi is capable of 50mph and the blue Tesco delivery van is a Ryton GM Mk2.

His future vision concludes with an elevated view of Kings Cross, with a hedge in the central median in place of today's railings and bendy trolleybuses added to the mix. No fossil fuels are used in any of the transport and Sunbeam's new SG2 trolleybus has atmospheric exchange technology added to its specification, allowing it to generate electricity by night and produce four times the amount it uses in service. ■

Above: **The Electric Boris in Oxford Street.**

Below: **Kings Cross 2033.** Pictures by ALAN PAGE

The buses of

The London Bus Museum has an unmatched collection of London buses, from the days of horse traction to the 1970s, on display on a wider museum site with much to offer the whole family as well as the most passionate enthusiast

T31, an AEC Regal dating from 1929, greets visitors as they enter the London Bus Museum.

Brooklands

London's transport heritage has been well cared for, both by London Transport in its various incarnations and by the London Bus Preservation Trust.

The public face of London transport history is the London Transport Museum at Covent Garden (see p130), and for the hardcore enthusiasts the name 'Cobham' was synonymous with London bus preservation, with bus owners and volunteers producing some stunning restorations in the cramped conditions of a disused World War 2 Vickers aircraft factory in that rather select corner of Surrey.

But the London Bus Preservation Trust (LBPT) had greater ambitions and in 2011 vacated the Cobham premises for a brand new building at nearby Brooklands Museum, the site of the UK's first purpose-built motor racing circuit and of many engineering and technical achievements throughout the 20th century.

Brooklands is a collection of attractions, including the Motoring Village and the remains of the famous banked racetrack, the fascinating Aviation Collection and Concorde Experience, and the newest addition, the London Bus Museum,

Awaiting its turn for restoration is RLH23, returned from the United States in 2012. Alongside is one of the current projects, a new replica body being built on 1923 double-decker NS174.

bringing together many of the LBPT's impressive collection of London buses. Not all, though, as some are in store, but the plan is to rotate exhibits to ensure constant variety.

In the 2,400sqm De Boer All Weather Hall, a structure that allows the internal space to be fully used with a fabric covering that keeps it light and airy, are over 30 buses on display and in the workshops ranging from two Victorian horsebuses to a 1978 MCW Metrobus, plus two chassis and two more buses undergoing restoration.

Visitors are welcomed by London General T31, a 1929 AEC Regal single-decker that was the first privately preserved London bus, and are led through the history of London buses by some excellent displays and full-size vehicles. Very early motorbuses are, unsurprisingly, thin on the ground but there is a chassis of a 1920 General AEC K type on display, which will receive a body in time.

LBPT also has solid-tyred AEC NS174 of 1923, which is undergoing restoration to its original open-top form, complementing covered-top, pneumatic-tyred NS1995 in the London Transport Museum collection.

Chocolate 'pirate'

Most of the buses on display at Brooklands are owned by LBPT but one that is on loan from noted private preservationist Mike Sutcliffe is the superb 1924 Chocolate Express Leyland LB5, representing the London 'pirate' operators, on display alongside 1925 Dennis 4-ton, D142 new to another 'pirate', W. H. Cook's Dominion Omnibus Company.

Next, fresh from a recent outing on the London-Brighton historic commercial

London Bus Museum, Cobham Hall, Brooklands Road, Weybridge, Surrey, KT13 0QN, open daily 10.00-17.00 (to 16.00 in winter), admission (to Brooklands Museum) £10 (concessions £9, children 5-16 £5.50, family £27).

Annual membership of the London Bus Preservation Trust costs £30 for an individual, £45 for couples and £55 for families (two adults and up to three children under 16). Members are entitled to unlimited access, free of charge (except for certain occasional special events), during normal opening hours to London Bus Museum and to Brooklands Museum. For further details phone 01932 837994, or visit www.londonbusmuseum.com.

vehicle run is ex-Thomas Tilling ST922, a 1930 AEC Regent that illustrates the great advances in bus design during the late 1920s, which led to the longer STL type Regents, with 1934 STL441 (repatriated from a museum in the Netherlands) and 1937 STL2377.

Representing London's pioneering engineering vision in the 1930s are 1935 side-engined AEC Q Type single-deck Q83 and 1938 rear-engined Leyland Cub CR16. A more conventional prewar vehicle is AEC Regal Green Line coach T504 of 1938.

The culmination of London Transport's 1930s design advances is a star exhibit, RT1, the prototype AEC Regent RT of 1939, a type that was set to go into squadron service but was delayed by the intervention of World War 2; deliveries in the postwar years took the total RT family to nearly 7,000 buses. RT2775, which famously toured the United States promoting Britain in 1952, is also on display.

A reminder of the war is provided by Guy Arab G351, a type that helped to keep London moving in these difficult

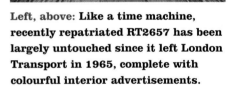

AEC Regents and a Green Line Regal from the 1930s. The breakdown tender is a 1933 Regent with a van body.

Left, above: Like a time machine, recently repatriated RT2657 has been largely untouched since it left London Transport in 1965, complete with colourful interior advertisements.

years, but actually a 1945 vehicle to a relaxed and less utilitarian specification.

While London Transport was developing its postwar standard single-deck models it bought proprietary types like 1949 Leyland Tiger TD95, before the appearance of the RF type AEC Regal IVs, represented by Central Area RF395 and Green Line RF226 of 1952. LBPT also has private hire RF19 and RFW6, and really just lacks a BEA one-and-a-half deck Regal IV to complete the set. An important exhibit being prepared for painting in the spacious workshops this year is UMP 227, the 1949 prototype of the Regal IV, Britain's archetypal postwar single-decker and father of London Transport's RF type.

The smaller driver-only buses in the Country Area were replaced in 1953 by the 26-seat Guy Specials, like GS34.

LBPT has a good selection of the iconic

The De Boer All Weather Hall forms part of the complex of museum buildings at Brooklands.

THE LBPT COLLECTION

SINGLE-DECK
1929 AEC Regal T31
1935 AEC Regal T357
1931 AEC Renown LT1059
1935 AEC Q Q83
1936 AEC Regal T448
1938 AEC Regal T504
1939 Leyland Cub CR16*
1949 Leyland Tiger TD95
1949 AEC Regal UMP 227
1951 AEC Regal RFW6
1951 AEC Regal RF19
1952 AEC Regal RF226
1952 AEC Regal RF395
1953 Guy Special GS34
1960 AEC Reliance RW3*
1971 AEC Swift SMS369
1972 AEC Reliance RP90

DOUBLE-DECK
c1875 'knifeboard' horsebus
c1895 'garden seat' horsebus
c1895 'garden seat' horsebus
1920 AEC K chassis
1923 AEC NS174
c1922 Leyland LB5 Chocolate Express*
1925 Dennis 4-ton D142
1930 AEC Regent ST922
1934 AEC Regent STL441
1937 AEC Regent STL2093
1937 AEC Regent STL2377
1939 AEC Regent RT1
1945 Guy Arab G351
1948 AEC Regent RT2657
1949 Leyland Titan RTL139
1949 AEC Regent RT chassis
1952 AEC Regent RT2775
1952 AEC Regent RT3491*
1952 AEC Regent RLH53
1957 Leyland Routemaster RML3
1959 AEC Routemaster RM140
1962 AEC Routemaster RMC1461
1968 AEC Routemaster RML2760*
1978 MCW Metrobus M6
1979 Leyland Titan T23

* On loan to London Bus Museum

The museum is an educational resource. Here, children learn about the oldest exhibit, a horsebus dating from around 1875 with sideways-facing 'knifeboard' seating upstairs.

Routemaster, including 1957 Leyland-built prototype RML3, early production RM140, Green Line RMC1461 and, on loan from Stagecoach, RML2760, the last example built.

More modern buses are not forgotten, and 1979 MCW Metrobus M6 is on display with its contemporary, Leyland Titan T23, in LBPT's satellite storage facility. Also in the collection, but not currently displayed, is a 1971 AEC Swift representing an unhappy episode in London's bus story and there are inevitably gaps in the collection that could be filled — perhaps an RTW type Leyland, a Daimler Fleetline, Leyland National, Leyland Olympian and articulated Mercedes-Benz Citaro.

Back from abroad
One gap was filled recently by the return in 2012 from the United States of an AEC Regent III lowbridge RLH type, on display as received and in the queue for restoration. Another more recent repatriation was RT2657, returned from the AMTUIR museum in Paris for the princely sum of €1 (plus transport costs) and still largely as withdrawn and donated to that museum in 1965.

Another gap has been filled by the loan of RW3, one of the AEC Reliances that gave London Transport its first taste of two-door buses.

Visitors to Brooklands Museum pay a single price for entry that allows them to enjoy all the attractions on the site,

an arrangement that Guy Marriott, chairman of LBPT, feels works well for everybody. 'Over 75% of Brooklands visitors call into the London Bus Museum, and that adds up to around 100,000 visitors a year. We also welcome school parties who learn a great deal about transport in their visits.

'We aim to tell the story of the London bus and this is of course a continuing story and it's important that as our collection grows we will need to reflect the privatisation of London's buses and on into Transport for London days.

'Running a museum of this size and scope with volunteers could be a challenge, but we have an excellent team of around 100 who do everything from specialist jobs in the workshops to stewards helping our visitors, to the curatorial team who meet weekly to catalogue and file our growing stock of photographs and other ephemera.

'By the end of 2013 we hope to have full museum accreditation, which only comes when you can demonstrate professionalism and a commitment to learning and education.'

David Kinnear, curatorial director, says Brooklands provides an ideal site for major events, where the previous Cobham events were spread over two sites. 'Our Spring Gathering was our most successful yet, with over 4,800 visitors, and we hold other events during the season — full details are on our website.'

From the cramped and increasingly unsuitable premises at Cobham, the LBPT

Filling one of the gaps in the museum collection is RW3, one of three experimental two-door AEC Reliances bought for London Transport's Country Area in 1960.

has taken a giant step towards ensuring that London's bus heritage is preserved for future generations to enjoy in an attractive and highly professional setting

and it is a tribute to all the volunteers who, over the past 40 years, have worked tirelessly to achieve this worthwhile goal. ■ **GB**

London Transport Museum

Many years before enthusiasts set off down the preservation route, London's transport operators recognised the value of saving representatives of important vehicle types from its bus, coach, tramway and railway operations, as well as examples of its world-class posters, maps and general signage.

A sample of these can be seen at the London Transport Museum, a justly popular attraction that presents the city's transport history in a very accessible and hands-on way in the former flower market at Covent Garden in the heart of London.

The importance of public transport to London's development is told through a series of exhibits and displays that capture the atmosphere of the city over the past few centuries. Good use is made of the restricted space at Covent Garden and though enthusiasts may miss the wider selection of

full-size vehicles that were an attractive feature of the museum when it was housed at Syon Park, and Clapham before that, for an all-age international audience the museum presses all the right buttons — something young hands are able and encouraged to do in the various interactive displays.

There may currently be just five bus exhibits — and one of the attractions is that the displays can and do change — but they illustrate the rapid development of the London bus. At the time of writing, the buses are B340 of 1911, representing London General's first standard double-decker; C94, a 1936 Leyland Cub single-decker; 1939 K2 trolleybus 1253; RT4825 of 1954, the last of London's RT family; and a representative Routemaster, RM1737 of 1963.

Enthusiasts wishing to see more of the buses in the London Transport Museum collection can visit the spacious Museum Depot at Acton on

The big-bonneted front of 1936 Leyland Cub C94.

Electric street transport represented by Leyland-built trolleybus 1253 and a 1910 West Ham tram.

one of the open weekends where a greater variety is held — an impressive 400,000 items.

London Transport Museum, Covent Garden Piazza, London WC2E 7BB, open 10.00-18.00 (Fridays 11.00-18.00), admission £15 (concessions £11.50, children under 16, free). For further details, including Museum Depot at Acton openings, phone 020 7565 7298 or 020 7565 7299 (24hr), or visit www.ltmuseum.co.uk

Part of the multi-level display area at Covent Garden, with RM1737 and RT4825 next to a 1938 tube train.